THE
UNIVERSAL PRINCIPLES
AND THE
METAMORPHIC TECHNIQUE

GASTON SAINT-PIERRE

BOOKS

Winchester, UK
New York, USA

Copyright © 2004 O Books
46A West Street, Alresford, Hants SO24 9AU, U.K.
Tel: +44 (0) 1962 736880 Fax: +44 (0) 1962 736881
E-mail: office@johnhunt-publishing.com
www.johnhunt-publishing.com
www.0-books.net

U.S. office:
240 West 35th Street, Suite 500
New York, NY10001
E-mail: obooks@aol.com

Text: © 2004 Gaston Saint-Pierre

Design: Nautilus Design (UK) Ltd

ISBN 1 903816 60 2

A CIP catalogue record for this book is available from the British Library.

Printed in Great Britain by CPI Antony Rowe, Chippenham, Wiltshire

THE
UNIVERSAL
PRINCIPLES
AND THE
METAMORPHIC
TECHNIQUE

CONTENTS

INTRODUCTION

This book is about the principles regulating the universe and ourselves. It will deal with the necessity, through these principles, to move away from the continual pursuit of change, showing that it is possible to dissolve the barriers preventing transformation. It will be useful also for people who want to find inner poise, to expand their consciousness by understanding the laws regulating their actions and life events, and to stop being at the mercy of circumstances and their fate. It will show that it is possible to embrace one's destiny by understanding the unifying factor at the basis of various strands, of light, matter, sound, breath and consciousness, in order to express an adult approach to life. It is therefore addressed to people willing to stop the headlong rush to the suicide of mankind through clumsy husbandry.

What pushes us to meditate or to contemplate? Is it an attempt at finding out who or what the programmer is? What if the programmer and the programme were one and the same thing, proceeding with an order that stemmed from principles established as the programme/programmer evolved? From these principles, laws would be deduced regulating the level of manifestations of this programme/programmer. These questions are asked from the desire to gain an overview in understanding the way the Universe works. But this book adopts a more grounded approach, looking at the actual nature of the principles underlying the very composition of the Cosmos and at the laws regulating it and ourselves.

These principles do not emerge from an intellectual vacuum, nor am I concerned to take credit for originality. There is little new in the history of ideas. Since the early 1970s I have become acquainted with some tenets of Hinduism, Buddhism, Islam, Christianity, and Western esoteric literature; I have also met religious thinkers, mystics, clairvoyants, and healers.

Some books in particular made a deep impression on me. For example, in 1982 I was given a sixteen-page leaflet, a resume of a book titled *The Kybalion*, written by "Three Initiates" in the early 1900s. The book purports to be a summary of the teachings of Hermes Trismegistus, the Greek name of the Egyptian god Thoth, who had received from the gods, several thousand years ago, a set of teachings that we might today call "transmissions". My imagination was fired as I realised that most of the content of the leaflet tallied with my own observations over the previous years. Ten years later, I was enthralled by a contemporary work, *Starseed, The Third Millenium: Living in the Posthistoric World* by Ken Carey, from which I quote extensively in this book. Readers may therefore already be familiar with many of the concepts I present, and I hope the text is accessible because grounded in our common spiritual heritage. At the same time, I hope that the specific configuration of ideas, and particularly the fact that they are, in a sense, embedded in life rather than in intellect, will be refreshing and vibrant.

It is probably helpful if at this stage I introduce the Metamorphic Technique, an approach to creativity, healing, self-healing, growth, and transformation, that I have been teaching since the 1970s. The technique is based on the fact that many of our life patterns, including ailments, behavioural characteristics and so on, appear to be implanted, in a kind of seed form, in our consciousness at the moment of conception. Through the gestation period in the womb, the individual begins to develop as a physical entity and as a moving being; the seeds of consciousness are beginning to germinate. Our normal life as children, adolescents, and adults is, in some sense, a flowering of the seeds. Yet in some people, for a variety of reasons, the flowering appears to be stifled. To change the metaphor, the caterpillar does not take to the skies on butterfly wings. Creativity may not manifest strongly. Problems, depressions, or illness may impinge on the individual.

The Metamorphic Technique often allows individuals to re-form their lives. It is a very simple approach to people, a kind of ritual performed by practitioners to meet the yearning for transformation of the people who go to see them. The hunger for food will make you go to the kitchen and prepare a meal or go to the restaurant. The ritual of eating is meeting the hunger for food. But what is most important happens later when the energy of the body transforms the food into itself. If the transformation were not done, of course we would die. Though the ritual has its role to play, it is not all-important in terms of transforming the food. The yearning for transformation pushes people to receive sessions of the Metamorphic Technique. The practitioner provides the environment to meet the yearning. People's life-force transforms their patterns, releasing the potential of self-healing.

Practically, at the physical level, practitioners touch specific areas of the feet, hands and head of the people who come to see them, creating an environment that is free of direction within which the power of life can move in a way that is right for itself. At a more subtle level, the practitioners act as catalysts, as the earth is a catalyst for the seed. As such they stay out of the way, practising detachment which is defined as noticing the facts, acknowledging their presence, and letting them be. People's innate intelligence guides their life force towards release of patterns, problems and difficulties, ensuring realisation of their potential.

I was instrumental in creating the Metamorphic Association, a registered charity, in 1979, to help promote Metamorphosis by providing sessions and instruction to the public, mainly through classes, workshops and lectures. This work has taken me all over Europe, to the American continent and Australasia, meeting all kinds of people. After sessions in the Metamorphic Technique, to many people's amazement, immediate physical or emotional changes can be noticed , reflecting, perhaps, the inner transformation of some life patterns, be it with Down's Syndrome or other learning difficulties. This transformation can take place at the subtle level so that it is hardly noticed by the conscious mind, occurring to people with a variety of psychological problems, and to thousands of individuals who view it as a simple, powerful, and joyous component of their journey through life. The Metamorphic Technique is now widely recognised as a respected adjunct in the field of complementary approach to health and healing.

As mentioned, the ideas in this book were developed in the context of my work with the Metamorphic Association. I am indeed grateful to practitioners and participants to my workshops who have stimulated and informed my thinking. The Metamorphic Association used to publish a Journal, and several chapters of this book first appeared, in earlier forms, in its pages. The practice explained in Chapter Eleven can be seen as an extension, or fruition, of the Metamorphic Technique. The Metamorphic Technique and the Universal Principles are sometimes taught in separate workshops, and sometimes together.

The ideas and practice discussed in this book arise from my work and personal observations over the past twenty and more years. For example, I once gave a three-hour workshop to a group of people with AIDS; their questions, insights, and awareness were of a unique calibre. Although they were not well exercised in the ways of discussing their innermost feelings, they raised questions and made observations that were deeply searching and to the point. For some of them, each moment was a matter of life or death. Some had to lie down to rest from time to time. They were confronting their own deaths in a very real way, but they were also there, in that room, with a willingness to delve deeper into the awareness of the ways their destiny was moving.

We stuck to the facts, not to mental projections, and questioned everything. Many of their fears, their desires, hopes, and their belief systems were laid bare within those three hours, and found to be of little use to them. And so, what was left? The question was asked, not out of despair and anxiety but out of a feeling of liberation: oh yes! I see now what is happening; I see I am dying - and that is a fact. We had reached the heart of the matter. There came power and joy, and a subtle current of love energy permeated the group. We had entered a matrix and it accommodated their likely death. Matrices or spheres, like beds of love, are there already, waiting in the wings as it were, at our disposal out of time, space, and matter. When we are aware of what is happening here and now, when we let facts be, then we align ourselves to what is; this willingness to align allows for communication between the different dimensions.

One pole of the group's state of mind consisted of fear, hope, doubt, resentment, frustration and defiance. By attending to its content and letting it rest, another pole appeared on the horizon of their consciousness. There was emotion for sure. A subtle joy, and understanding of the value of patience and tolerance, a smiling sort of loving, objective care. By embracing both poles they became aware that, beyond the so-called positive and negative aspects of the situation lay the source of the power to transcend it.

The professional approach to AIDS work was in its infancy at the time of the meeting. The invitation to present my work "The Metamorphic Technique", which was briefly discussed above, had come from someone who had understood that the transformation can happen in all sorts of contexts, be it in the pursuit of creative activity or at the threshold of death.

From such encounters my own consciousness was gradually enriched and I developed a number of ideas which were constantly checked in my work. From the above, for example, I observed that through a conscientious exploration of one aspect of a polarity, its other aspect may emerge, sometimes in a blinding light that transforms one's vision. I began to formulate a set of principles that are described in this book as Universal Principles, since I found them to be of relevance in so many spheres of life: emotional, personal, intellectual, philosophical. In fact, they seem to operate as a kind of law implicit in our life here on this planet. By understanding the nature of these principles it is possible to benefit from them by aligning ourselves consciously to their dynamism. If we abide by the laws of the country in which we are staying, we will have a harmonious and peaceful sojourn. Becoming aware of laws that regulate us here can make our stay on earth a pleasurable and productive experience. We become sensitive to a subtle equilibrium pervading our nature. Furthermore, this awareness ensures our full presence in the solar system as cosmic beings.

I am not putting these ideas forward primarily for conceptualisation, nor as any contribution to the history of ideas. They arise from life, and my proposal is, if any reader should find them worthwhile pursuing, that they should be evaluated in the reader's own life. Perhaps because of my many year's involvement with the Metamorphic Technique, I am deeply convinced that our consciousness can and should be focused, stimulated and empowered. Reading and philosophising contribute to this awakening. But yet another dimension can come into play when the awakening is embedded in our physical and cellular being. This claim may appear strange if one is unaccustomed to working with energies at the level of light, cellular biology, and consciousness of the Void, which accompanies transformation and plenitude. My suggestion is that, as one can see the Principles operating in daily life, so one will experience them at a profound level by following the practice outlined in this book. Again, my basis for making this statement is through observations made at numerous workshops and subsequent correspondence with participants. The way to test it would be to try the technique for oneself.

I should perhaps state that personally I have no specific religious or philosophical affiliation, although I have the deepest respect for our mystical heritage as it has surfaced in many cultures throughout the world. This book does not conform to any religious or philosophical paradigm. Nor does it aim to dispute or contradict any particular viewpoints. I sincerely believe that a believer in any religion or philosophy, or an agnostic, or an atheist, might find it stimulating but not confrontational. Are there any key ideas that run through the text? Through the years of teaching the principles, I have realised that many people find it helpful to bear in mind the following: one is to nurture and to trust absolutely the power of life, or the life force. The power of life in each of us has infinite capacity to transform, to heal, to guide, to break through barriers. If we were truly open to it, we would not have the slightest need of religious professionals, of healers, psychotherapists, clairvoyants or anybody else. Our problems arise precisely because somehow we have cut ourselves off from our source. We are light, yet the world often appears dark. We are constantly living in truth, in a world of facts, yet somehow we surround ourselves with falsehood.

A first implication of this attitude is that we should always attend to the true facts of a situation, as far as we can fathom them, rather than divert our attention down side-alleys and by-ways. I am searching for the bright light of truth, not for comfort. An AIDS patient may be dying. That is his or her truth. Transformation may come after exploring that truth; it is unlikely to arise by avoiding it.

Also, it appears to me that this life of ours is, one might say, governed or regulated by the principles I identify. As mentioned, our sojourn here may be more fruitful if we are aware of them. Now, five of the principles I refer to are as "within the domain of space, time and matter". (Students of Indian philosophy may equate this with the domain of name and form.) These five are gender, causation, correspondence, rhythm and polarity. Thus these principles are to be found in the material and biological world, as well as in the more subtle and complex arena of human relationships, emotions, and ideas.

The remaining principles - vibration, creative impulse, insight/illumination, communication/communion - I consider to be "outside" this physical universe. They operate in and from a transcendent dimension. We may say they have no material base. Yet I notice, and I believe readers can experience it, that they make their presence felt here. And as we feel the presence, it manifests in a way that is increasingly powerful. Of course the relationship between the transcendent and the material, soul and body, God and creation has pre-occupied humanity for thousands of years. In some spiritual traditions for example Sufism and Tantra, all distinctions collapse. The dualistic conceptions of sacred or profane, outside or inside the physical world, are transcended. Yet these categories remain used and useful as modes of explanation, and for some spiritual practices. It is in this spirit they are used here. So in the text we move back and forth between our daily world and more subtle realms.

Our mind encompasses a double vision. At times we feel a presence or power that we may call God. Then we are prayerful, we experience the joy of worship, or the bliss of communion. We pray to our Father in heaven. At times we have the feeling that this "God" is a wave on the surface of a vast ocean of blissful consciousness. If we could dive deep into the ocean, we would find in some profound sense an identity between our consciousness and the divine consciousness. My Father and I are one. The greatest mystics have pointed to this experience, and at this point they reach the boundaries of language.

In my work, I meet so many instances of self-inflicted

restrictions. And once we accept limitations on ourselves, we constrain those close to us. Actually, as far as I have been able to discover there are no limits to our consciousness. There are no limits that I have been able to discover to the consciousness in anyone, so-called "with learning difficulties" or otherwise. But as long as we persist with our own learning difficulties we feel as if restricted. The feeling of constraint is inevitable, but transient and illusory. It is imposed by ourselves and to be dissolved by ourselves.

When we consider ourselves, when we look at the universe, we see nothing but change in matter, forces and mental states. Nothing endures but change. This realisation produces a need and a yearning for permanence and continuity but as we go on exploring deeper into our own psyche, we realise that all of these changes must be but outward appearances or manifestations of some greater or deeper realities. As we go on delving into the mysteries, the separation between whom we understand that we are and whom we feel that we could be becomes obvious, creating some psychological insecurity from which we try to distract ourselves either through games, superstition and belief systems, or — as is current today — through psychic activities, religious and spiritual pursuits. We exacerbate the yearnings. Attempts to reach outwards or inwards — God out there, God within — produce misery and occasionally the belief in our puritanical society that life, to be worthwhile, must be difficult. At times, by a supreme act of imagination, we lift ourselves out of that misery and, like the climber at the top of the mountain who sees very intricate networks of roads among which some of them lead to the peak, we unveil a map that can bring us to a greater understanding of what we are beyond who we are and of the nature of the universe that we reflect.

The core of this book comprises nine chapters, each of which discusses one 'principle'. As mentioned, some of the material first appeared in the pages of our Journals from the mid-1980s onwards. The nine principles are gender, causation, correspondence, rhythm, polarity, vibration, creative impulse, insight/illumination, and communication/communion. In each case I offer a more or less theoretical account of what I mean by the principle, and sometimes draw parallels with similar ideas in religious or philosophical literature. I also illustrate them, usually with accounts of my own personal experiences and those that I have heard about in workshops or amongst practitioners and friends. I would like to emphasise that the principles emerged into my consciousness from living rather than from reading. Nevertheless, books have been useful as points of comparison and, sometimes, clarification. Each chapter ends with a short summary. My hope is that each reader would like to approach a chapter with an open mind to make of it what he or she will. But then perhaps it would be useful for me to restate in brief some essential points that I am trying to make before embarking on the following chapter.

There remain two important chapters. In one, I attempt a kind of synthesis, to show how the nine principles relate to each other, their mutual dynamism and interaction. I also discuss some topics that relate to the Universal Principles as a whole rather than to any one in particular. The other chapter is an outline of the practice that has been developed to bed these principles into one's being so they may become a lived experience rather than only mental furniture. Of course it is rather difficult to learn something like this purely from a text, and I hope that any reader whose interest is aroused may one day like to join a workshop to study in more detail. The chapter should also be a useful reference section for those who have attended workshops.

It may be helpful for the reader to have a general idea of what I mean by "the practice". In brief, we have identified reflex points on the feet, hands, and head that correspond to seven of the nine principles. The physical body is here considered somewhat as a canvas, on which a beautiful picture may be painted. Our "artistic technique" is a quiet communion, usually with a partner, with each of the relevant reflex points. Two of the nine principles may be considered truly "transcendent", in the sense there is no obvious way to approach them or get at them even through subtle gestures relating to the physical body. They are supra-human. I have the intuition that probably the pituitary and pineal glands are also somehow related to the transcendent principles, and that there is a resonance with the realms of light, inspiration, and the Void. If these are not yet available through the physical or subtle body, at least we may begin to intuit them through the practice.

CHAPTER ONE

Enlightenment is biological fulfilment at the cellular level

The principle of gender is active in everything. Every thing and every person contains within itself, within himself or within herself the masculine and the feminine aspect of this principle. Gender manifests on all planetary levels, within the realm of matter and energy and therefore of polarity and duality. The very atoms which constitute matter have within them their electrons with their negative charge and their protons with their positive charge. Matter is our springboard and the principle of gender is one of the necessary elements of creation and creativity.

Evolution itself goes from simplicity to complexity, with the forms that are created eventually exploding under their own "weight", to be shattered into simple units which, in their turn, become complex. And so the dance goes on. The many different myths of creation throughout the world illustrate the same process: elements of a basic but complex fabric detach themselves from it to embody qualities that will take them to a different level of manifestation.

Forms arise, evolve and disappear, freeing energy which then manifests in yet other forms. It is noticeable that certain basic elements, which have a definite relationship with each other, and are brought together by the frequency of the vibration at which they function, always constitute these forms. The form may be a galaxy and the elements may be the stellar dusts, other forms may be a crowd of people, a liver with its multitude of cells, an acorn or an amoeba. Their materialisation in time and space implies polarisation within them of specific forces, and such a relationship can be described, according to the viewpoint as attraction/repulsion, positive/negative, or masculine/feminine: the relationship seems to be the result of the action of these forces. Though the forces within a form may not appear to be active, they will be found to be so at another level of manifestation.

Forms are the product of a convergence of forces with a specific organisation. The death of a form is the dissolution of that specific organisation, the energy from which goes on to fuel another type of organisation, at a level in harmony with yet another convergence of forces that, in its turn, allows other forms to arise. Animal faeces mixed with straw foster a multitude of living organisms that, as manure, nourish and regenerate the soil and are "generators" of new forms. The convergence of forces is brought about by another of the Universal Principles, Mentalism or the Creative Impulse, which we will discuss in chapter 7.

Matter is an expression of consciousness at a specific level of vibration. Is it possible to accede to another realm of consciousness through the exercise of duality? Raise the frequency of the vibration and another expression arises, which in the case of humans is consciousness of consciousness.

The so-called "fall" in the Hebrew book of 'Genesis' is one account of the entry into matter and form of a new level of consciousness previously unknown to humans. The potential of knowing that one could know was actualised, as the consciousness from the animal-human to the human-human became activated. We went from the state of knowing as animals do, to the state of knowing that we know. Far from being a "fall," it was the start for humans of self-reflective consciousness. The "coming out of Paradise" refers to the superseding of the animal consciousness of the humans as the realisation of a different level of consciousness dawned. In other words, animals, plants and the human body as such may well be conscious at an elementary level but as human/humans we are conscious that we are conscious.

The principle of gender is, as stated before, in everything. For example, in a gathering of any organism, balance can be found between the active and passive elements, some elements expressing more at one point than another their masculine or feminine aspects. Within each of us we find these two principles at work, whether it be in our tendencies at different times either to "make things happen" or to "let them happen."

Will is an expression of the masculine principle while imagination and intuition express the feminine. The masculine aspect within each of us stimulates and energises creativity while the feminine aspect generates and brings to fruition, helping to develop into maturity what the masculine has seeded. There is mind as opposed to sensitivity, active versus receptive, the ability to perceive and the ability to respond with consciousness.

When there is union between a man and a woman,

resulting in the creation of the zygote, that very cell is the product of the complementary genetic structure of male and female. Hence it follows that within each one of the trillions of our cells are the pairs of aspects, masculine-feminine, active-receptive, positive-negative. Considering the principle of gender is similar to considering the cloth from which a suit is made. The cut of a man's suit may differ from that of a woman's, but the cloth is the same. In other words, the "cloth of matter" manifesting as a cosmos, or a protozoon or an atom, contains within itself the masculine and feminine aspects in unity. Remember that gender manifests on all planetary levels. Perhaps we could say that the "cut" of a galaxy may be male or female but that the "cloth" of the galactic matter contains within itself both the masculine and the feminine aspects!

The only way in which we, as human beings, can understand the dynamism of the principle of gender as it manifests in us, is through the filter of our own consciousness. First, there is the physical being of the person expressed, at a gross level, as the body and its parts, and at a subtler level as energy, mind and emotion. Then, there are the matrices from which that physical being- be it mental, emotional or corporeal- has issued, such as consciousness and active forms of vibrations, which operate on a global level as a deep symbiotic communication or communion. On these different levels are to be found subtle and varied expressions of the principle of gender.

It is therefore difficult to keep our exploration strictly within the realm of time, space, matter, and energy, and hence of polarity and duality. This is because we find that gender is present in everything and more specifically in two abilities immediately present at the moment of our conception, which are developed during the nine months of our gestation: the ability to perceive consciously and the ability to respond with consciousness to what is perceived.

It is important to bear in mind that these two abilities must be integrated within ourselves in order for our lives to be in balance. A woman may function more actively from one aspect than from the other and so of course may a man; the result in each case is imbalance. If the person's masculine aspect is dominant, their task will be to discover and integrate their feminine aspect in order to express a harmonious state of being. Conversely if the feminine aspect is more highly developed, a person should look to their masculine side to create balance. Someone may, for example, be aware of certain patterns without exercising the ability to respond to them. On the other hand, they may respond automatically to a situation without necessarily being aware of the inherent factors that allowed it to arise. The ability to perceive with awareness is here equated to the masculine aspect of being and the ability to respond to the feminine aspect.

As integration is achieved between the masculine and the feminine, mind will be operating alongside sensitivity, intellect will allow emotion to have its say, animus will be friendly with anima, and there will be room for both linear and spatial approaches within the field of creativity. In other words, the tendencies in each one of us to "make things happen" or to "let things happen" will be well represented. It would be an error to favour one aspect as opposed to the other, as each of them has a necessary property – the masculine aspect, to stimulate and energise creativity and the feminine aspect to generate and bring to fruition or maturity what the masculine has triggered, to let go of it and act with its magnetism to call forth the new trigger of the masculine. The first, giving the ability to conceptualise, acts as an activator while the second, giving the ability to respond, manifests the principle of action as movement.

With integration, the pattern of balance and harmony seems to be reflected not only in the behaviour of the person, but also in all the cells of that person's body and specifically in the genetic structure given by the father and the mother. This balance is not, of course, a static state but a dynamic ability to remain poised between two poles; in this active equilibrium, if neither the masculine nor the feminine is emphasised at the expense of the other, the position of inner authority is achieved.

The word "authority" comes from the Greek (autos) meaning: "self, one's own, by oneself, independently", together with the suffix "ity" meaning "state or condition". The extended meaning is "affirmation of self". The self referred to here is the one arising out of the energy of the integration of the two parts of our nature, masculine and feminine, nourished by the energy of the earth and, through it, of the cosmos. It is vital for the foundation of our being to be well established, if we are to realise our potential as human beings. As people recognise the importance of being themselves, they discover their fundamental right to be.

We will study in chapter 3 in the principle of correspondence that everything is reflected in every other thing. It is logical that symbolically the principle of gender should be reflected in the lower part of the body, from the base of the spine to the feet, as it is through that part that the powerful energies of the earth may find entry to the body. They become active in man and receptive in woman and are awakened at puberty and made ready to fulfil their functions, which are for the man to stimulate and energise and for the woman to receive and bring the seed to maturation. If the principle of gender is well harmonised within the person and the point of entry for these energies is opened and functioning fully, then the body can be well sustained and the person will find completeness or totality within himself or herself, irrelevant of the sexual orientation, or whether that person belongs to a so-called sexual minority, or is celibate. A more refined type of energy that enters the upper part of the body from above the head can unite with the basic earth energies, refining and transmuting them. We will speak more of this in chapter 7.

"People who have achieved this psychological state are now able to work equally successfully through their masculine and feminine energies, will be constructively independent in their work and consistently successful in their relationships with both men and women because these will not be based on need."[1] This might well result in the state of androgyny that has been witnessed in some of the great mystics. However, the belief that it is necessary, in order to reach the heights of creativity, to withdraw from the world, go to the mountain peaks, become ethereal and shun matter, is a false one. More often than not this results in exaggerated traits of personality and lack of creative output. However, this does not deny the validity of withdrawing from distractions that the mind is only too keen to cultivate in order to assert its control. The importance of being grounded can not be over-emphasised. The perennial question is how.

We contain within ourselves the very pattern of deep-rootedness, of being grounded, which was established during the first three months in our mother's womb. This is called the cephalo-caudal development that arose when what became the spine issued out of the mass of energy that became the head and the brain. The development is therefore from the head to the base of the spine. Being aware of the presence of this pattern within our cellular memory, and at the same time attending to the fact of our lack of groundedness, while just letting that fact be, produces an intimate type of communication between the pattern and the fact. And this communication pushes us, without effort, toward discovering the appropriate exercise, the right attitude of mind, the different mode of behaviour that will gently allow us to incarnate more fully. This is of paramount importance if we are not to find ourselves at the mercy of one of the tyrannies that the mind exercises – the tyranny of experience and memory where the energy is used in the mindless repetition of patterns of the past. Caught in the cycles of manifestation, we enter into a state of resonance with another type of tyranny enacted on a universal scale, the tyranny of form with its attendant entropy of habit.

In a slightly different context, let us look succinctly at the revolutionary ideas of the plant physiologist Rupert Sheldrake[2] on what forms are and how they influence our behaviour.

"What Sheldrake suggests is that the Universe does not so much have laws as habits. Everything that happens in fact sets up an invisible matrix or morphogenetic field, a formative causative field creating a tendency for other things to happen in the same way. In other words, habits. One of the examples that Sheldrake uses to demonstrate this phenomenon is the breaking of the four minute mile record in athletics. Up to the time Roger Bannister succeeded in doing this it was generally regarded as impossible. However once it was achieved, very quickly other athletes followed in Bannister's footsteps, each strengthening the original morphogenetic form enabling future athletes to succeed more easily."[3]

Consciousness is a vibration, with a frequency that is faster than the speed of light. (This consciousness can be called objective and must be distinguished from the everyday type of subjective consciousness with which we live our life). As this frequency slows down to a rate that is slower than that of the speed of light, manifestations of life such as matter, emotion, mind, time and space, appear. These will tend to deflect the energy toward the reproduction of themselves and toward the repetitious enactment of dualistic forces that the law of gender seeks to implement at this level, resulting in the negation for humans of the creative impulse that belongs to the level out of time, space and matter - the level faster than the speed of light. The mind tries to encompass these two levels, but cannot do so as they are mutually exclusive when experienced.

"The mind has enormous potential to see the similarities between two things but the perception of essential differences will quite often escape it. It is the essential differences between two things that separate them totally and the similarities are then seen to have been purely incidental. Another strange aspect to what we refer to as essence is that if you remove one percent of it and attempt to retain ninety nine percent, you are left with none of it. Such an action leads inevitably to the destruction of the essence."[4]

Is it possible, without enjoying the support and the comfort of any form, without recipe or programme - which would kill the creative impulse - to integrate the elements that constitute the basis of our nature in order for us to go beyond them and realise our potential as human beings, in order to birth ourselves? This question demands a radical solution which includes the cessation of the emotional links between children and parents. The genetic structure at the very heart of our cells was given to us by our parents. We are truly of our parents. Their union produced the child that we were. The realisation of our potential as human beings, however, is the emergence of another type of child.

As the spermatozoid and the ovum united, these two cells died to themselves to form the zygote. So must the emotional ties that link us to our parents cease to exist, so that the energy they divert may be used to integrate the past contained in the genetic structures of father and mother at the very heart of our cells. We must come to terms with the void that our parents protect us from, warding off, as they do, the atavistic terrors arising from the nights of time.

The desire for our perpetuation into the future with which we burden our children must also cease, yet another void.

We must heed the injunction that Khahlil Gibran puts so beautifully in The Prophet:
"Your children are not your children
They are the sons and daughters of Life's longing for itself
They come through you but not from you
And though they are with you yet they belong not to you"

This does not mean that parents and children cannot remain friends, but they must be free from the emotional projections which leach those very energies that our life force can use to actualise our potential and shape our destiny in accordance to its own cosmic necessity. But what can happen when the emotional energy is thus economised?

Physicists now seem to agree with the mystics in saying that matter is crystallised light. The new child that one can be is therefore the light-being springing from the very heart of the cells. The emotional ties are cut so we become our own father and mother and truly parent the emerging child. By parenting ourselves, we may become transparent. Could it be that enlightenment is nothing more than a biological fulfilment at the cellular level?

Summary

A principle of gender, or duality, appears to pervade every structure. One may point to electron and proton in the atom; male and female in organisms; sun and moon in our heavens. There are many subtle and varied expressions of this principle in our lives.

The terms "masculine" and "feminine" are suggestive only: these energies are not restricted to men and women respectively. On the contrary, it is a fundamental task for each individual, man or woman, to integrate the two aspects. Unbalanced manifestation of one or the other tends to sterility.

Masculine energy makes things happen: it pushes towards action with will and determination.

Feminine energy lets things happen: it is responsive, brings things to fruition, acts through intuition and imagination.

The masculine involves the ability to perceive, to view, to be detached; while the feminine expresses the movement of active caring. It is important to remember that the cut of the suit may be different for a woman than for a man but the cloth is the same.

To achieve balance within the gender energies implies resonance with the earth. In the physical body, this resonance is associated with the feet and legs. Hence the importance of being "grounded" or "rooted". The integration of masculine and feminine leads to a secure inner feminine foundation and inner authority.

CHAPTER TWO

The Universe has generated you to appreciate its beauty

As you sow, so shall you reap. Every cause has an effect, every effect is the result of a cause. This is the principle of causation, one of the universal principles that has influenced the human mind for thousands of years, through the ancient Hindu and Buddhist philosophies right up to the way our minds work today. The attempt to explain everything, from the movement of the planets to the inner workings of the body according to this clockwork syndrome, has been based – until now with the discoveries in the new physics – on the law of cause and effect that derives from the principle of causation.

The mechanistic understanding of the universe and the human being, prevalent in both physics and medicine in the past centuries, has been adopted by the mind in order to satisfy its need for certainty and proof, which is to be found in the law that the effect follows the cause. The order in the universe could thus be explained. The warning of Poincaré, the French mathematician and physician, that the accepted explanation was not necessarily the truth, was not heeded.

The principle of causation has been used, since the beginning of history, as a basis for the understanding of the passage of time.

"...As long as we live in the past, we are subject to the law of cause and effect which leaves no room for the exertion of free will and makes us slaves of necessity. The same holds good for what we call 'dwelling in the future,' which generally is only a state of reversed memory — a combination of past experiences, projected into the future. When, however, the past or the future are experienced in clairvoyant states, they become present which is the only form in which we can experience reality (of which the other forms are so to say "perspectively distorted reflexes"). Only while dwelling in the present, i.e., in moments of full awareness and "awakedness", are we free.

Thus we are partaking of both: the realm of law or necessity, as well as the realm of freedom. . ."[5]

The Old Testament tells us that the union of Adam and Eve, the symbols of the first man and the first woman, produced children who in their turn united to produce more children, and so on to the vast human population of today. Through our ancestors we are the product of the first man and the first woman. And our children in their turn are the forbears of future nations. A firm belief in the progression of time from the past to the future has thus become established in the human mind

Since time immemorial generations have come and gone, lived, borne children and passed away. We are the effects of their actions and what we do today will affect future generations. Every thought we think, every action we perform has direct and indirect results that are links in the great chain of cause and effect. We may say that something has happened by chance, but we are then merely expressing our ignorance of the cause from which it arose, which we are unable to perceive or to understand. Everything happens according to the law of cause and effect and what we call chance is simply an instance when the law is not recognised.

This principle is the one which dictates that every thing affects every other thing. Up until recently our understanding of the world kept us captives of this causal chain of events. Now however, we have at our disposal the energy to free ourselves of that determinism through the principle of correspondence, as we begin to realise that everything may indeed affect every other thing in the same way that the reflection in the mirror of an image will be altered as the image changes.

One factor, which has been available to mankind throughout the ages, enables us to free ourselves of the chains of cause and effect. It is love which allows us to reach the level at which the frequency of our basic vibration operates; that awareness will help us bring to the surface the experiences that we did not face fully in the past, experiences which were using up a lot of energy to sustain their presence. This may also help us to face the experiences that we are busy running away from now. Love allows us to complete "unfinished business," therefore freeing energy that will be used to deepen our perception of reality and attune us and refine our being.

Love in practice can be experienced through detachment, which I would define as noting the facts, acknowledging their presence and simply letting them be. It is through that love that, as catalysts, we realise the importance of staying only with the facts that we perceive, without looking for explanations, without interpreting, without attempting to direct the energy of the facts in any way whatsoever, in other words of keeping well out of the way. Then the energy, be it in the form of a headache, a mental handicap, a sexual yearning or an overwhelming feeling of happiness, can move of its own accord and reveal its potential. This is not only a non-interventionist philosophy but also a practical way of operating in the world. The energy of the facts, when it is not appropriated by the mind, can then bring about action that is spontaneous and creative.

The energy of one level, thus freed, can create new forms at another level. This then involves a deep morality, of right actions performed at the right time at the right pace and in the right way and it has nothing to do with mind and its limitations. Our love is such that we agree to let the facts be. The block of ice cannot reach out to water, in a manner of speaking, but the more enlightened consciousness of water can encompass the block of ice. The bridge is established not from the lower to the higher but from the finer to the grosser levels.

My closest friend in England drowned while she was on holiday. I was shattered. A few hours after hearing the news, I realised I could choose the level of consciousness on which I could face the event. I could remain at the mercy of the grief and the feeling of emptiness, or I could ride that energy by staying with the facts. I chose the latter course of action : "Joan is dead. That is a fact. I will never see Joan again. That is another fact." By simply considering the facts as they arose, there was the awareness of the coming and going of the waves of emotion. At times there were tears, grief and deep feelings of pain welling up, while I was walking along the street, talking to a friend on the telephone, or being quiet for a few moments. These were facts to be acknowledged and to be allowed to be. A profound objective love was present, coming partly from the energy of the truths that the facts were, partly from my willingness to be attentive to the facts. A communication was established, at a level other than that of mind and emotion. And the love underlying it called forth many incidents from the past that had been buried, forgotten or dismissed, and these childhood memories of separation, of betrayal, of forgetfulness on the part of adults and parents, of broken promises, could be redeemed and released.

* * * * * * * * * *

The principle of causation has been construed as an absolute but of course it is not that. Humans came to this conclusion as they evolved the ability to perceive the unmanifest moving into the manifest. The limitless potential of the unmanifest is curbed and whittled down when its energy becomes manifest. The manifest is regulated by principles operating in time, space and matter and bound by the laws derived from them, namely the laws of gender, correspondence, rhythm, polarity, together with the law of cause and effect. This last one is illustrated at its most earthly level in the sexual act. Through the coming together of man and woman in the act of love, the spermatozoid and the ovum extend the means by which the new potential life may manifest as the child.

With human beings, the union of a man and a woman "causes" a child to be conceived. The principle of gender explored in the previous chapter teaches us that the masculine-feminine aspect is an inherent part of the fabric of this new being. The body, by its nature, is actually materialised patterns from the past, which can be found in the genetic inheritance from the father and the mother. So with the law of cause and effect we can see how the principle of gender comes into play.

As both parents unite their genetic structure exercises a material influence on the "purity" of the energy manifesting as a new life. In its turn this material influence attracts non-material influences that are "pockets" of consciousness and energy in time and space but not in matter. These are the products of "unfinished business" as it were, of lives and thought forms or images that may be called karmic patterns, something we will consider later. These two types of influences – material and non-material – will come to, or be present in, the new cell at conception, attracted by an affinity with the specific way in which this being will fulfil its purpose on earth. They will determine the whole make-up of this new life, rendering it unique.

Influences and tendencies are aids in one's life, but they must not be regarded as absolutes. The cloth of a suit is not to be confused with the person wearing that suit. And yet, in its slowness to grasp the essence of a human being, the mind has done just that by taking the existence of these influences as the basis for explanations of reincarnation that are prevalent in some parts of the world. Some of the elements that will help us to fulfil the purpose for which we have come to earth may actually be those that still need to be worked at. What are they and from where do they come?

When someone dies, the organisation of the various structures which constitute that person ceases to exist and so the energy inherent in the organisation leaves. It returns to the pool of energy or life from which it issued in the first place. The body disintegrates and its matter returns to mother earth. If they have not been able to reach completion the subtler forms of the physical, which are projected mental structures – such as desires, hopes, fears, strong belief systems, unacknowledged passions, appetites for power and control, social convention and traditional values – will continue in time and space, which is visible time from the past. If these projected mental structures had reached completion, they would not remain.

We can feel this subtle form of the physical when we visit an ancient place of worship. The atmosphere that we sense is usually made up of two elements: the first is the power coming from the particular ground on which the temple or the cathedral has been built; and the second is the living power of life of all the worshippers who have projected their emotional needs and their prayers, usually part flattery part demand onto the deities of the site. The influences that this subtle form of the physical exercises are neither good nor bad; it depends on our standpoint at the time whether we turn them into so-called positive or negative effects. Above all, they need the structure of a body to become functional.

As I said it is at conception that the genes of the first cell provide the structures of the past that attract the non-material influences that have an affinity with this new existence. However, this cell is not only a precipitation in time, space and matter of these two types of influence but much more importantly, a manifestation of the particular life and intelligence that has slowed down the frequency of its vibration in order to "appear." Full incarnation is therefore the bridging in awareness from the power and the consciousness which are the children of life and intelligence, to their greatly stepped down physical counterparts, matter and mind in an act of love where emotion releases its need for direction in a communion of all levels.

* * * * * * * * * *

"A man is the creator of his own fate, and even in his foetal life he is affected by the dynamics of the works of his prior existence . . .

This human body entombs a self which is nothing if not emphatically a worker. It is the works of this self in a prior existence which determine the nature of its organism in the next. . . What is lotted cannot be blotted. A frightened mouse runs to its hole; a scared serpent, to a well; a terrified elephant, to its stake but where can a man fly from his Karma?"
Garuda Purana, CXIII[6]

"... In India, home of so much speculation, many schools developed and debated the subject, each with its own viewpoints. One influential school (Samkhya) developed a typical "incarnation model": a plurality of eternal souls, of a totally different substance from the world of nature (mental processes, interestingly, were classified as belonging to nature, not soul). The soul enters flesh at conception, and comes into this world of sorrow, where it remains through an endless cycle of rebirths, until it can attain liberation through understanding its essential non-material nature.

There are countless variations on this theme in different traditions: after death the soul may immediately recycle, go to heaven/hell; rebirth may be animal, human; the soul/consciousness may depend on past actions/lessons learned, have individual continuity, arrive freshly every time, have tenuous connections with other lives, and so on.

The variations could be subtle and complex: for example some Buddhist schools denied the continuity of individual consciousness, but suggested some kind of link between a person on the point of death and a life about to begin for example, if a person dies while still in the grip of delusion and desire, the new life will start in this state also...."

"...A materialist would probably identify with his body, or more probably with his money, and consider all theories about incarnation as nonsense. Many religious believers might identify in some way with a soul, a super-physical entity which transcends bank-balances: thus, they may envisage a happy life for the soul after, or even in the midst of, physical hardships. Perhaps most religious systems tacitly or overtly accept a version of this 'soul in matter' concept..."

"...I wonder if, in some way, it is fear that lies behind, or plays a part in, some of man's ideas about incarnation. He experiences himself as an isolated, separate entity, and then tries to trace back a separate starting-point and individual, life-line; the question of individual origin naturally concerns him greatly. Perhaps a deeper insight into wholeness would allow us instead to see the flowering of life into thousands of forms every instant: trees, machines, humans and animals creating new situations in an unbroken stream. Thus the new viewpoint, universal rather than personal, might lead to an altogether different way of experiencing the world. Conception, incarnation may be now, not thirty or fifty years ago."[7]

Law and necessity are at the basis of instinct, that wonderful mechanism that takes the burden from the level of mind and matter, of having to decide on a course of action when biological perpetuation is at stake. It implies a level of behaviour that is free from the pedestrian process of analysis, logic and reason, a level of behaviour where connections are made that go against everything we have learned in the past and everything we have experienced or stored in our memories. It is a way that consciousness chooses to express necessity without having to rely on our slow mental activity.

The instinct of survival is common to all instinct-based events, but it is a movement of being that external circumstances, imposing undue pressures on it, can deregulate. The mind is the culprit here as it channels the energy of the survival instinct towards the protection of the ego. As the ego is capable of using only ten percent of the brain's capacity natural norms are destroyed and imbalance ensues. Over past centuries the mind has tended to apply itself more and more to the investigation and study of the material world, channelling its vast reservoir of energy into cul-de-sacs. Fascinated by its ability to unravel truths whilst at the same time limited by its poor perceptual abilities, the ego has been unable to fathom the higher frequencies of the heart energy. The language of objective love is not understood in the ego's subjective and divisive world.

Whereas mankind has discovered how to unleash the tremendous power at the heart of the atom, forging for itself the potential for total destruction, it has however not been able to deal with the problem of over-population where bigotry, wilfully cultivated ignorance and "feudal" belief systems inhibit self-regulatory factors such as the use of contraception, programmes of education and attunement to the profound rhythms of the body.

Instinct is to be found at the interface of consciousness and mind. Where consciousness is predominant, material values may be forgotten, but if mind has the upper hand, the material imposes its weight, and the lightness and immediacy of insight and understanding are blurred by learning through experience and the accumulation of knowledge.

I was having breakfast with a friend one warm summer

morning, on the terrace facing the large garden. There was a state of suspension, highlighted by the play of a young cat running all out after flies just stopping a millimetre away from a large bay window. Then, it would dart in another direction, the play of instinct and enjoyment delicately poised. The gardener appeared, pushing a wheelbarrow full of garden tools. He stumbled and scattered the tools on the path, making quite a din. The three of us jumped out of our skin. My friend and I watched as the young cat started playing again, running at full speed after another fly. It crashed right into the window pane, almost knocking itself out. Fear, a mental attribute, had clouded its perception. The past was now intruding, curbing the freedom of its play. Fear and mind veiled the cat's consciousness, so that it hurt itself.

The law of cause and effect may be considered as one of the many influences that help us fulfil our potential as human beings. It is not, however, an absolute in itself. When his disciples asked him: "Master, who did sin, this man, or his parents, that he was born blind?" Jesus answered: "Neither hath this man sinned, nor his parents: but that the works of God should be made manifest in him." Really he was saying that the law of causation was not at work in that man's case but that a purpose had been served out of the framework of time, space and matter.[8] So we must distinguish between cause and effect which is operating within the realm of time, space and matter, and a purpose that the mind cannot comprehend. The cause of an ailment may be eradicated through therapy, but if the purpose for it has not been fulfilled, it will reappear in one form or another.

As we have allowed materialising influences that are appropriate in the atomic and subatomic domains and in the subconscious human processes to dominate human endeavours, the dynamic movement of the principle of causation has moved from simplicity to repetitious habit, the direction of least resistance. This leads on to a movement of expansion which, if it is left unchecked, becomes proliferation to the bitter end. It is said that, if human beings were compared to the cells in a human body, the current rate of growth of the actual population would be considered as terminal cancer.

The reach of human consciousness is expanding to such an extent that we are beginning to realise within ourselves the awesome task set out by the intelligence that we really are: to contain within our embrace both the temporal and the timeless, the spatial and the spaceless, the world of matter and the formless. We know we could cross the threshold of light and come back, and yet our shyness and our delusion that trivialities are important prevent us from claiming our inheritance. We must reverse the process of the sequence of cause and effect through consciousness in order to connect with what we are truly. The paradox lies in the fact that by embracing our fate, we are led to the fulfilment of our destiny, and by embracing duality we would put an end to its dominance, establishing the ground from which unity flowers. Ovum and spermatozoid, instead of remaining in the bodies and nourishing them with their energies, absorb themselves in each other and lose their "identity as organs", creating a human being, one person. The union of the masculine and the feminine principles at the heart of each cell "causes" a new "child" to be born, the crystallised light that is the matter of the cell decrystallising to reveal light in all its purity. Cells can thus birth themselves. Union is therefore the ultimate aim of creation, and accomplished in consciousness that is the sole purpose and the only reason for human beings on earth. Creator and creation can be One.

This dynamic movement is also what is at the source of habit with its tendency to go on repeating the same patterns. It takes the light and the energy of a greater consciousness to force the cells out of the patterns of a disease for example that they will otherwise go on sustaining, because their elementary consciousness is subject to the dynamism of the law of cause and effect. If the cells break free from this force of habit, instead of proliferating and dying, they may be able to realise their potential of light. Could this biological fulfilment be the forerunner for illumination?

Poised between habit which is influenced by memory and our potential, is it possible to stop revisiting the past when we look for an answer to the question: why? Instead of answering the question, "Why did you do that" with the words "Because she told me to", or "Why did you listen to her?", with "Because she knows and has experience", we can invite our potential and answer the question 'why' with the words 'in order to … ', then act accordingly.

The intervention of consciousness reveals a wonderful mystery. Just as the potential of a human being lies in the first cell created by the union of the spermatozoid and the ovum, so in that very cell is also buried a greater potential of fulfilment, as light, if consciousness is used to awaken, to shape and to organise this potential. There are two cycles present. There is the natural one that is fixed and repetitive, where the energy within the cause can be seen to motivate or generate its own transformation. From an acorn comes an oak that will produce acorns from which oaks will grow; out of a caterpillar forming its chrysalis will emerge a butterfly, not a monkey! The other cycle entails a movement of consciousness that lifts the energy of the fact onto another dimension where the principle of causation no longer has any sway because we are now out of the level of duality and mind that separates and divides. Cause and effect become one, united in purpose and necessity. Light is light is light.

The direction of the dynamic movement of the principle of causation does not always however happen from the past to the future, from cause to effect. We usually look to the past to discover the cause of our diseases. It might be wise to look in the future too, as very often the effect precedes the cause, something which happens when two levels of activities are mixed.

If we consider only one level of activity, then the effect follows the cause. For example, if you work today, you will be paid tonight and that will enable you to buy some food with which to satisfy your hunger tomorrow. If however we mix the two levels of activity: working and thinking, then the effect may precede the cause. "If you think you will be hungry tomorrow, you then think you must work today in order to buy some food." Then you seek work today, so that the reason for the work is the fear of hunger tomorrow. Looking at it this way sheds a new light on our behaviour: you may, for example, want to take a break from work in a week's time but for one reason or another do not feel able to request it. That wish may trigger a state of ill health this week so that you feel justified in taking that time off without feeling guilty.

When the causative chain is broken, the void that ensues may bring out fear or sadness or boredom or desolation in us as the patterns of the past, that were serving as reference points, dissolve. Forbears can be blamed no longer. The mindless repetition of patterns is seen as empty ritual. The endless battles against pain and illness cease.

If we apply this to the level of everyday human existence, a totally different type of behaviour arises in relationship. The energy which was previously put into the sublimation of the sexual desire can now be used to fuel the body of light that we begin to express spontaneously. A feedback phenomenon occurs that draws cosmic energy to feed and regenerate this "cocoon" of light. The sexual union of two people partaking of that energy, if it occurs, can no longer be the product of need but a celebration. Without one partner being defined by, or seeking to define, the other partner because they are both total in themselves, there is freedom. Adulthood is manifest in this differentiated monism. There is unity in diversity.

There is an irreversible movement that begins to occur, not only at the individual level mentioned above, but also at the level of the organs of the body of humanity, each one with a specific task fulfilling in their own manner their part of the purpose of that body, be it a group of people, a nation or a race. The eastern philosophy of karma adopted the reincarnational standpoint that what one does in the course of each lifetime will affect subsequent lifetimes. An echo of this is to be found in a different form and at an extreme level in excessive concentration on materialism and technology which is rampant in the Western hemisphere and spreading throughout the world. However, this movement is being checked by the natural emergence of an energy whose dynamism belongs to a different dimension from the one at work in the principle of causation with its characteristic linear determinism. We are moving from this approach to a global perspective, from the linear approach of causation to the global one inherent in the principle of correspondence which we will discuss in the next chapter.

If we consider the principle of correspondence it may be that through affinity to our actions we attract to ourselves characteristics that have nothing to do with the effect of these actions. This means that what happens to us may not necessarily be caused by previous action but may simply be a reflection of the vibrational energy rate and the level of consciousness at which we are functioning. There may also be an affinity with part of the purpose for which we are here on earth, which is to express consciousness of consciousness. We do indeed have the ability to know that we know, which is also the prerogative of subtler realms than the one we inhabit. However, our purpose is to incarnate that ability in the domain of time, space and matter or form, which cannot be done in the subtle realms.

SUMMARY

The principle of causation refers to the "law" of cause and effect. This concept was known to ancient philosophers of various cultures, and it is a plausible explanation of many phenomena: one event causes another in a determinist chain, operating in sequential time.

Much Indian philosophy is based on the concept of karma, the working out of the consequences of actions in individual lives, as, for example, a bad deed gives rise to a bad effect. The philosophy also encompasses a search for the dimension beyond karma, where cause and effect are transcended.

The vast edifice of modern technology, and the conventional Western worldview, is built almost exclusively on a determinist, causation-dominated philosophical foundation. One can indeed discover causes for many events; if one fails to discover an adequate cause, conventional thinking assumes that a cause exists but is at present unknown.

While the concept of causation is helpful in many contexts, it is intrinsically limited. Rigid belief in causation can become a prison. Can we move from the realm of causation and determinism to the realm of creativity and freedom? Can we move from our time-bound habits, repetitions, and memories, to realise our potential?

A restricted view of our individuality assumes that all the elements of our being come from the past – perhaps genetically coded into the first cell of our embryo, to be played back in later life like the music on a pre-recorded cassette.

Metamorphosis implies that the first and subsequent cells provide only a structure, a material base, that may attract new energies, events, and awareness at any time.

These factors may break the chain of causation. Consciousness and light are never bound by the past; on the contrary, when they break into our awareness they over-ride all previous programmes. They may wipe the cassette and instil a new music.

CHAPTER THREE

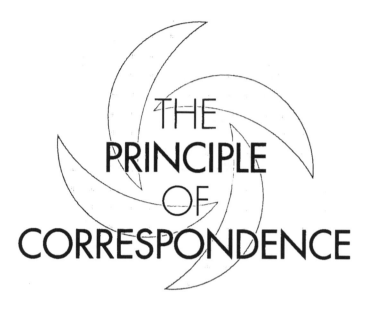

THE PRINCIPLE OF CORRESPONDENCE

Love is our ultimate mirror

The principle of correspondence states that everything reflects every other thing and is perfectly expressed in the ancient hermetic saying: "As above, so below; as below, so above." More recently, the Swedish philosopher Emanuel Swedenborg (1688—1772) stated in his Doctrine of Correspondences that every natural object symbolises or corresponds to some spiritual fact or principle that is, as it were, its archetype or prototype. His tenet was that the Scriptures were written in harmony with these correspondences.

There is however an even more exciting facet that can derive from that principle. It gives us a hint, not only of the nature of the universe and of ourselves, but also of the essence of the underlying power that sustains both. Through the study of the principle of correspondence, we can unravel the progression of the unmanifest to the manifest, of simplicity to complexity. More importantly, if we reverse this process, we may gain an understanding of the unifying factor underlying reality and realms beyond it.

Historically, a shift is taking place as important and radical as when the influx of oxygen, hitherto almost absent, allowed aerobic creatures to live in an environment no longer hostile to its survival. It killed off most of the anaerobic creatures in the process.[9] A balance in the atmosphere ensued, and we benefit from it today. The shift concerns a movement of energy and consciousness whose frequency is accelerating, beginning to be regulated less by the law of cause and effect as it comes more and more under the influence of the dynamism of the principle of correspondence. Hence the importance of investigating the nature of that principle.

We may be reaching a climax in our human history, a completion of the adolescent phase of the body of humanity, a moment of fulfilment that allows us to open the door onto a new perspective, the one of adulthood. All that has gone before might be merely the particular phase of a gestational cycle presiding to the development of a planetary intelligence that is still too large a concept, too broad a vision for those cloaked in cultural bias to see.

This shift has been in the making for quite a few thousand years, being prepared and announced on the more subtle levels of vibrations and reaching down now to the level at which we live our everyday life. The last throes of the principle of causation have been marked by an over-emphasis on the part of humans on materialism and laws related to it, commercial, political and economic, mechanical and gravitational, electrical, magnetic and thermal to name but a few. An ingenious use of the law of cause and effect has triggered off the explosion of technological expertise. The lamp on the table sheds its light and this is an outcome of a long line of relationship of cause and effect, starting with the water in some far-off river activating turbines to create electricity. Through the principle of correspondence, instead of harnessing power in the above fashion with the attendant cost to the environment in terms of pollution and ecological disturbance, and also to one's pocket cost, why not learn to tap directly the freely available power in the isotopes of water, for example? Couldn't the tremendous explosion of the means of communication with its global interaction be replaced by the everyday use of telepathic contact?

If we want to know the universe, we have simply to know ourselves. The key to everything that is lies within each human being. We are in essence a copy image of every other human being. We are a variation of the manifestation of the principles that regulate the universe. In the play of mirrors it follows that to know yourself as an awakened individual is to also know yourself as a being reflected in the surrounding context. To know that context is to know the cosmos and the underlying factors allowing the existence of its being.

The principle of correspondence allows us therefore to proceed from the known to the unknown. Indeed, if A corresponds to B and B corresponds to C, then A corresponds to C. Or to put it more prosaically, if a kilo of apples cost £1.00 and a book has the same price, then we can exchange apples against book directly. The state or condition of agreement of things or of one thing with another that this principle expresses, is the foundation of mathematics and science. In their study of matter, scientists go from the known to the unknown, projecting, conjecturing, extrapolating, inferring, deducing, practising lateral thinking and so on. The equations necessary to measure the distance between the earth, the sun and the moon, and all the calculations allowing the footprints of an astronaut to be imprinted on the surface of the moon, stem from the fact that scientists deduct the unknown from the known, the assumption being that the known is a mirror of the unknown.

The ancient Chinese knew of the links between parts of the body such as feet, hands and head being the mirrors of inner organs; this art has recently been put to use in what we now call reflexology. A recent discovery has found that the spinal reflex points of these organs correspond also to specific moments of the gestation of a person, from conception to birth, bringing in the space/time continuum and its subtle type of physicality to the domain of matter and energy. All the characteristics that were established during that period, at the physical, mental, emotional and behavioural levels, are those with which we live our life now. The book "The Metamorphic Technique"[10] describes also that, by looking from another angle, the skeleton, soft tissues and fluids correspond to specific aspects of human existence. More precisely, the hard tissues reflect the energy aspect of the person, his or her power, and at a deeper level are symbols of the life force of that person. The soft tissues in turn reflect the mental aspect and consciousness, and at a deeper level the innate intelligence. The fluids correspond to the emotional aspect, to feeling and communication, and further, to the ecstasy in the movement of creation. The body is no longer therefore merely an organisation of the patterns of the past, the mental activities are no longer the product of experience, memory and association of bits of acquired knowledge, the emotions are no longer energetic arousal searching for expression. This means that when we touch one another, shaking hands, embracing, giving or receiving a massage, making love, we are truly getting in touch with the power of life, the innate intelligence and the ultimate emotion that is creation manifesting as that person. In its materialistic bias, the mind tends to reject the beauty of the dynamic truth within the principle of correspondence, afraid of its inherent glory and power.

To adopt another approach, let us consider the principle of correspondence from a transcendental viewpoint. There is life and intelligence whose action is creation in the infinite, the eternal and the absolute. These three facets of the ultimate Oneness "slow their movement down" to express, out of time, space and matter or form, power and consciousness whose action is communication. (This is the first level of reflection). (See Chapter 9 — The Principle of Communication/Communion.) This abstract domain is nevertheless specific vibrations out of which comes the realm of matter, time and space, the world of physicality manifesting as energy, mental and emotional structures. (This is the second level of reflection). These will be reflected in the human body as bones, soft tissues and fluids respectively. (This is the third level of reflection). The bones constitute the corporeal structure that the soft tissues help to move, the organs ensuring the functioning of the body. (This is the fourth level of reflection). This movement is far from being chaotic as it is imbued of a direction given by the fluids, the formative matrix at work in all new manifestations of life, and the source of order. Along the bony ridge on the inner side of the feet, the thumbs and along a medial line from the top of the head down to the base of the skull, where the spinal reflex points are to be found, these areas reflect also the prenatal pattern, i.e. the nine months of our gestation period when the totality of our characteristics were established. (This is the fifth level of reflection).

For Emanuel Swedenborg, the detailed process of evolution and diversification of life forms present in nature's kingdoms, mineral, vegetable and animal is representative of man's inner development.

"The living mind is beautifully represented in the three kingdoms of nature. The mineral kingdom contains the representations of the 'building clocks' of the mind, the strong, constant, factual elements that are a necessary basis for any thought or developing wisdom. The vegetable kingdom represents the mind developing with living thoughts often reaching great heights and branching out in all directions like beautiful trees, and multiplying indefinitely, as one thought leads to another. Finally the animal kingdom mirrors forth the mind teeming with warm blooded affections and desire which move out to touch other persons in a living way.

However, nature sometimes reveals another face — harsh, fierce and destructive. This is reflecting back distortions and degeneration in man's mind."[11]

The embryonic division and differentiation of the cells of a new human being as well as the theory of recapitulation whereby we experienced in mother's womb the different stages of evolution of nature's kingdoms, clothes and reflects the inner development of our subtler nature, providing us with the templates and the basic patterns for the realisation of our purpose.

"As civilised man turns back to his own spiritual resources, now that he is beginning to find scientific technology bankrupt as a source of deep happiness and fulfilment, so he needs to rediscover and develop his knowledge of the eternal, the phenomenon of representation which, in itself, has never ceased to operate in nature and in man's dreams. Once again, he can be in touch with, and begin to comprehend life at a deeper level, and so find that meaning and purpose which is, perhaps, the one fundamental drive of the psyche which underpins all his aspirations and endeavours."[12]

The scientists can perceive that there is a relation of congruity between the orbital of an electron around the nucleus and the orbit that planets trace in space. Or that the movement of the atom is a reflection of the movement involving the Universe. And one not only reflects the other but can affect the behaviour of the other in an intricate dance of evolving forms.

The exploration and experiments of the scientists never bring about transformation from one level to another. Inventions and discoveries are simply the logical extension of the things that are known. The mathematical equations allow the scientist to create an aircraft and to put human beings on the moon. Throughout the equation there is an expansion and a projection from the known data that stretches the mind and the understanding into grasping what was hitherto hidden, secret or not revealed.

Understanding and knowledge may affect the quality of one's life, but ultimately it does not transform anything. The discoveries of the scientists do not change them at the human level. They remain prone to the same type of conditioning, emotions and attitudes of mind.

The principle of correspondence regulates the activity that allows everything to go from one state to another, or from one form of organisation to another form. It points to the fact that within all forms there is the potential of every other forms, even providing the energy for these new forms to manifest. However it doesn't of itself create the new forms, presenting a reflection of these forms and their inherent potential with lesser or greater accuracy in accordance to the viewpoint adopted. As a piece of a hologram image is enlarged, it is seen to contain the whole image but with a hazy resolution. As we return closer to the source of light, the laser beam, the woolly outlines become sharper. From one standpoint we are the fuzzy reflection of the ultimate power.

This is also exemplified from another angle in the form of expression that is called language. The word "chair" is analogous to the piece of furniture on which I am sitting. Language is nothing but the stringing of symbols through a display of thoughts, feelings, emotions and concepts. Indeed, the whole of the language system is a direct expression of the principle of correspondence. A concept in itself is the repository of a power that can very easily create a lack of flow if the mind prevents this principle of correspondence from instilling its dynamism. If I say the word "table," then immediately all the shapes and forms that are representing a table come into mind and become fixed as a form in potential that will occupy a place in space with a definite duration in time. However if I banish the word "table" from my vocabulary, then I can consider everything that has a flat surface on which to deposit something as a table whether it is the floor, the earth, etc. The word "table" is the expression of a specific limitation in time, space and matter.

To give a name to something is to fix it, in the process providing us with a feeling of possession. The spell that language exercises is perpetuated through generation, enshrining a level of perception and affecting our understanding, a theory for example becoming an accepted truth until a different level of perception invalidates it. Linguistic permutation gives us the illusion of deep understanding but most often a play on words, a joke does not translate into another language. We are only too keen to define our inner world and to describe it with the biases, failures, inadequacies and blind spots of the originator of a theory, especially at the psychological level, thereby burdening ourselves with the limitations of the consciousness of its inventor, and using our energy to make forms that fit the system. A Freudian analysis will produce a Freudian type of dreams. The greatest type of understanding, the one without knowledge, concepts or words is denied to those who adhere solely to verbal, conceptual understanding and are happy to drown in a sea of words and information.

The story of Helen Keller however, demonstrates the dynamic potential of the world of concepts. Blind, deaf and dumb, her sense of touch only was used to put her in contact with water under different forms, running, stationary, cold, warm, splashing and so on, while a friend would help her trace the word water with a finger. The eventual understanding that a similar gesture referred to various forms unlocked her mind to the potential of language and abstraction, allowing her to live a successful, rewarding and inspiring life henceforth.

Dreams use the language of correspondence in sleep to create order in the mass of data that assault our senses everyday. However, as mind and ego are mostly at bay, little energy is usurped or spent to impose control and exercise power. That energy can then be used to bring to the surface of the consciousness, even though one is asleep, intimations of deeper levels of our being with which we may commune directly; or it may take the form of encounters with personified aspects of ourselves or with discarnate forms as a way that we use to impart to ourselves a message, a teaching whose time has come, and so on. We gain access thereby to levels of being that we are, to as many facets of the one and only being that we are, denied to our ordinary everyday type of consciousness. Ultimately, continuity of consciousness throughout day and night can be achieved through attention and the power deriving from the exquisite alignment to the energy of the universal principles.

Arts, poetry, music, painting, the great visionary works, constitute as many keys able to unlock levels of the human psyche that hesitates at the threshold of dimensions where the mind with its physicality has no access. Through the principle of correspondence, the energy of attention may take us into uncharted territories, triggered off by the beauty of a work of art or the strange excitement due to some resonance of vibrations. What has happened? A note, a sound, through its harmonics, has set off your own basic note, and the signature key of your being, for one timeless moment, resonates to a cosmic vibration.

The principle of correspondence is the foundation of rituals and religions to which they owe their existence. They are keys created and used by the human mind to intimate the presence of dimensions or worlds beyond the grasp of that mind. The Christian mass celebrated in remembrance of Christ's Last Supper uses the principle when the priest affirms in the name of Christ: "This is my body" while showing a piece of bread. The voodoo minister uses also this same principle when sticking needles in a doll's body representing someone in order to cause a specific course of action to happen. The intent of these two people is all that matters.

Myths, legends and fairy tales remind us of the need of our unconscious side to express itself by taking on representational forms from nature. The emergence of the same underlying themes in different cultures demonstrates that they may originate in a deep common level of the human psyche.

"Long before Freud and Jung, Swedenborg came to perceive that the Bible was the spiritual psychological history of man's universal spirit, and that the ancient myths were other forms of the same thing, modified and sometimes distorted by the various cultures through which they had passed."[13]

"Myth has been dismissed — even *defined* — as primitive superstition by a youthful, scientific culture whose extraordinary rapid success in the material sphere had gone to its head. But now myth is in the process of being reinstated as the respectable vehicle of the unconscious, conveying not primitive understandings of the external world, but man's universal sensing of his own inner world, much of which now lies unconscious for most of the time. Thus it is now possible to see the Bible itself as true myth, the vehicle of a revelation of the spiritual psyche in its total development from start to full completion. Because so much of the Bible is truly historical, its real purpose as 'myth' which conceals and can reveal universally experienced inner spiritual states and stages, has been missed in our historically minded era."[14]

Most of the myths and legends comprise an element of journey, of going at the discovery or to the confrontation of something in order to unveil hitherto unknown aspects or levels of awareness of the protagonist. The Greek hero Hercules deliberately sought great challenges to come to terms with himself. The rites of passage of adolescence are a reflection of the necessary integration of our animal instincts to free the energy for the human realisation of our potentials of creativity. We need to unfold the secrets of our existence buried in our originating depths. The human body and its unfoldment in the womb hold quite a few keys.

In the human body, the solar plexus, i.e., the area between the base of the rib cage and the navel, reflects the principle of correspondence. It is indeed through that area that we monitor the processes that are changing the world, "sensing" our close environment, especially when strong emotions are projected towards us, creating the proverbial 'knot in the stomach' or 'butterfly' type of occurrences. There is also a series of correlation that points to the solar plexus as being the most likely receptor and reflector of the energies of the principle of correspondence.

From the premise that everything reflects every other thing, we can see that the spinal reflex points on the feet mirror also the prenatal pattern, i.e., all the elements, physical and of consciousness, established in the nine months spent in mother's womb. There is a parallel evolution of the physical and consciousness aspects of our being called the prenatal pattern taking place then, so that when we were born, there was not just a live physical lump of matter coming out of the womb but the baby that we were, conscious and able to express feelings, emotions with a unique type of behaviour.

To look at it more closely, the prenatal pattern is composed of three main periods: from conception to the eighteenth week approximately called post-conception; from the eighteen to the twenty-second week called the quickening; from the twenty-second week to the moment of birth called pre-birth. During the first period of post-conception, mother and foetus are still at one physically while in terms of consciousness, the 'seeds' of our humanity and individuality (from the Latin *in dividuus*, that is to say 'without division') are 'planted' in the ground of our true self, a diffuse type of consciousness then, which will allow us to recognise the unifying factor at the basis of everything. The behavioural pattern of undifferentiated monism is thus established. If the embryo could reflect, it would say: "I am you". The patterns of this period will be re-enacted in life during babyhood and early childhood. Post-conception is reflected in the body from the throat to the solar plexus area.

During the second period, of quickening, mother feels the movements of her foetus who has become autonomous, its organs having started to function in earnest from the fourteenth week on. In terms of consciousness, there is the experience of opening to the world, the experience of duality, of consciousness of self and of something other than self or no self that will become the egoic faculties. If the foetus could speak, it would say: "I am different from you!" the typical reflection of the adolescent about to leave home to go at the conquest of the world. This period is reflected in the solar plexus.

The third period, of pre-birth, sees the foetus respond to external stimuli, establishing its aptitude to be in the world, its social beingness in terms of consciousness, while at the same time preparing itself to act, that is to be born. The behavioural pattern of differentiated monism is established, whose meaning is that we are one in our diverse attributes, that we are as complementary cells in the huge body of the cosmos. This will constitute the main quality of true adulthood. This period is reflected in the lower part of the body.

The first articulation of the big toe on the feet reflects the first cervical vertebra and also the moment of conception, (see a further explanation of this in the book "The Metamorphic Technique"[15]), then up to mid-arch is found the reflex points of the seven cervical and the first to the nine thoracic vertebrae, which also reflect the post-conception period. At mid-arch we have the reflex points of the ninth to the twelfth thoracic vertebrae, approximately the area of the solar plexus connected with the quickening period of the prenatal pattern; from there to the top part of the heel bone are reflected the lumbar vertebrae and the sacrum, the lower part of the body, the area also reflecting the pre-birth period. The top part of the heel bone on which attaches the Achilles tendon reflects the coccyx, the reflex point also of the moment of birth.

The period of the quickening, between the eighteenth to the twenty-second week is therefore, within the prenatal pattern, the time when the consciousness of the foetus opens itself to the world. Up to the fourteenth week it has been in a way, concerned only with self, undifferentiated, at one not only with mother but also with the cosmic energies that form its being. Then the foetus begins to move in the womb, opening up its perceptions to the world that is other than self, the wall of the womb. It is the period when the organs of the body have started to function fully. The foetus is now wholly in possession of its abilities and were it to be born, the baby could survive.

We have seen that this period is connected with the solar plexus. In that context, the solar plexus can be compared to a room or passage, a threshold, even a diving board in action. It represents one of the main veils that need to be lifted if a human being is to live a fully conscious life. That veil covers a fount of energy that will allow a person to go, in terms of consciousness from the perception of self to the perception of others. It is the hinge between the qualities of individuality and of social beingness within each one of us. It provides the energies that allow for the regulation of, and the equilibrium between, the masculine and feminine aspects of our being.

If relationship with self is well established in the post-conception period, and in life during childhood, then the relationship with other than self will be one of unity in diversity, the passage having occurred without undue difficulties. The exercise of the ability to be attentive and to respond to others can be entered into without any problem.

The warrior mentality is connected with the adolescent behaviour of opening to, and conquest of, the world. To explore, to test and to push further the boundaries of the personality and ego formation needs the awakening of emotional energy, which is readily available to the person's emergence of the consciousness of newly found powers. It is legitimate at puberty and shortly past it to be caught or be seduced by the exercise of power for a period but if it befalls an adult or a nation, aberrant types of behaviour may follow as these people have greater means at their disposal than the lonely teenager. Warrior nations are well known to curb dissident and enlightened understanding.

At the dawn of adolescence, the sensitivity of the child must enlarge to take on the new type of perception and awareness, awakening together with the sexual urge. The reference points have disappeared. New ones have not presented themselves yet. This void swallows everything. Innocence is lost, the childhood joys are no longer sufficient to palliate the need to find your place in the world. You are suspended between two worlds, the one that is fast vanishing and the other, limitless, dark, where you wander aimlessly. What you responded to up until now, beautiful landscape, felicitous poetry, what moved you to tears, appears now lifeless, empty. In its attempt to assert supremacy over the emerging power, the ego will push the teenager into the use of violence, self-mutilation or even suicide.

Responsibility and justice are elements of our being forged in the fire of the dynamic movement of the principle of correspondence. The word 'correspondence' comes from the Latin *cum respondere* whose etymological meaning stands for 'to warrant, to promise or pledge with'. This brings into light a particular ability connected with humans, which is conscious responsibility. Animals will look after their young in response to an instinctual drive. We can choose to do so and to provide our young with more or less loving attention or we can abstain, warping that drive. It is important to make clear the difference between 'taking responsibility' and 'being responsible'. The two actions are performed at completely different levels altogether. In order to take responsibility, one has to project through one's mind a goal after having perceived a course of action. This movement will always be limited as the mind is limited. Being responsible means exercising one's ability to respond in the moment to whatever facts or situations arise in actuality; it implies a keen alertness of the fact and a willingness to let the fact be, allowing it to find its own direction of release or transformation. We know that the power of the fact is sufficient to transform it from within. This also means a non-attachment to any particular form or structure, be it family, religion or nationality. "Who is my mother, my father ... etc. said Jesus.[16] There is therefore justice in action as events reflect the level of consciousness at which we choose to operate.

The principle of correspondence is also connected with compassion whose meaning, from the Latin *cum patire, to suffer with,* could be extended to 'my passion for life with your passion for life.' There is again a need to differentiate between 'having compassion' and 'being compassionate'. 'Having compassion' is simply an expression of one's need to help and has very little or nothing to do with the other person or the true external need of the moment, while 'being compassionate' is simply recognising the facts of another person and letting these be, knowing that the energy thus economised is there when and if an action is necessary. This action then is a creative act and has nothing to do with the activity of helping, or doing something for others. Compassion therefore also means justice because there is a recognition of an essential equality in the relationship thus established. "We are always in a context of our equals and the justice of love is always perfect."[17] At a mundane level, the plate of a scale will reflect what there is on the other plate.

I feel there is a great release of energy and of knowledge and a corresponding response to it taking place at the moment. Indeed there is a quickening replicating the one that we experienced in mother's womb at four and a half month. The pattern of awakening is inscribed at the very heart of our cells. Looking at the principle of correspondence is a way of being informed of the universal mysteries. Many veils are being withdrawn from many so-called esoteric teachings to allow the exchange of meaning and dialogue.

The earth and its inhabitants are bathed in, and are receiving, subtle energies from a dimension to which it owes its origins. Not only are we undergoing a new birth process but also we are beginning to receive a new type of mother's milk, so to speak, the solar system rooting for the cosmic breast. The solar plexus is truly acting as a cosmic receptor as the cosmos informs it of a new rhythm, of a different heartbeat.

In our study of the Universal Principles, which regulate the cosmos and everything perceptible by the human mind, we have discussed the principles of gender, causation and now of correspondence. We have found, in our research of the nine Universal Principles, that these three just mentioned constitute a triad most concerned with matter, time and space.

SUMMARY

The principles of gender and causation are widely understood and accepted, rooted in the material world and our daily experiences. With the principle of correspondence we move to more subtle levels, less mundane, more mystical.

The key to this principle is the idea that everything in the cosmos is interconnected; every thing reflects every other thing. This insight has implications that shatter "common sense". Earlier philosophers used the expressions "As above, so below" and "microcosm equates to macrocosm" to convey these ideas.

Correspondence may be used in healing. For example, in reflexology different internal organs are "reflected" on different areas on the soles of the feet and action directed onto these areas has an effect on the organs. In the Metamorphic Technique we have found that the weeks of quickening of the foetus correspond to the solar plexus in the physical structure, and adolescence in the temporal structure. Increasing sensitivity to this principle leads to responsibility and compassion.

The principle of correspondence may be linked to the idea of passage, the transformational movement from one state to another. For us, as humans, the passage is often mediated by symbols conveyed through language, dreams, rituals, art, or music. Although the symbols are apprehended by our senses, they point the mind away *from the world of the senses. Potent symbols are in effect messengers from territory that is, to us, unknown and uncharted.*

Parts of the human body are acknowledged as powerful symbols. Throughout Asia, the religious aspirant touches the feet of his guru to receive blessings; the greatest gurus touch the feet of their disciples to awaken the divine consciousness within. In the Metamorphic Technique we touch others' feet and awaken the power to transform.

If we are now at a turning point in human history, we may say it is accompanied by a surfacing of the principle of correspondence: a shift from linear to global consciousness. The search for perfection or contentment by investigating "things" out there needs to stop. Instead, we may consciously, and reasonably, aim to know the universe by knowing ourselves.

CHAPTER FOUR

The breath of life is
our true rhythm

The word rhythm comes from the Greek: *rhein*, which means to flow. Everything is in a state of flux, of movement, everything has a beginning, moves towards its peak and then declines. Just as the breath, with the rise and fall of the rib cage, is an echo of the ebb and flow of the tides such movement can be seen in everything, from the birth, life and death of the tiniest creature to the rise and fall of empires and civilisations. This is the principle of rhythm. The pendulum moves towards one extreme of its swing and then towards the other. These extremes are called poles. This movement occurs even in the feelings and changes that we notice in ourselves. Through simply being aware of these 'swings', we can arrive at a state of equilibrium, as rhythm creates an ever finer and shorter swing. By extension, within the principle of rhythm, we find that the movements neutralise themselves as the oscillations become faster and closer, producing the secondary principle of neutralisation, occurring at the point where the poles meet and merge.

Our study of the universal principles gives us an opportunity to harmonise with their dynamism. As I have already mentioned, if we go to an unfamiliar country but we know its laws and customs, our stay there can be happy, comfortable and harmonious. Its people's traditional ways of doing things and of being are likely to nurture us and to provide us with new insights, thereby deepening the understanding of our own humanity. Adapting our behaviour to a different rhythm can be challenging and unsettling but, if we are attentive and embrace the uncertainty that the new situation provides, then we may be greatly enriched. If we know the laws that regulate the universe and we abide by them, then we may stand to experience a pleasant stay in the universe. It seems that we have reached a point in our evolution where we have to embrace in consciousness the uncertainty which is connected with the changes in the universe and therefore with our changing position in it. If we are to survive the new influx of energy that pervades the solar system, brought about by such events as the shift from the Piscean Age to the Aquarian Age, we also have to agree to love that state. It is in love that true knowing abides and it is in love that the creativity stemming from the finer dimensions of our being can be revealed.

"Threads of earthlight, moonlight, and starlight weave the finely textured fabric of this galactic arm, interwoven here and there with tracings of another and eternal light, trails of a Presence passing, drawing with them into the future, the beauty, the majesty, the pageantry of unfolding Creation. We feel in this fabric, in the passage of these millennia, the steady splashing of waves, the pulse of rising tides and tides withdrawn."[18]

Nature presents us with analogical movements as we compare cosmic rhythms to life cycles; the four times of the day – midnight, morning, noon and evening – will be echoed in the seasons – winter, spring, summer and autumn – within which the eight phases of the moon cycle points to a distillation of a light reflecting journey in space. The full moon gloriously reveals itself as the total reflection of the sunlight, having progressed from the first crescent of the new moon through to the last one. From the seed of a plant to the flower that will crown it, we find first an expanding movement with its intense cellular explosion producing larger and more intricately designed leaves until the flower unveils its colours and frees its perfume pervading the environment like the solar rays of midday. Then, after fertilisation, a contracting movement will allow, through concentration, the maturation of the fruit and the formation of seeds bearer of the new plant, the fruit having dried out. And the cycle starts all over again.

What is the relevance of the principle of rhythm to our everyday lives? The uneven rhythm shown on a brain scan indicates sickness. The baby will be consoled and quietened by its mother's rhythmic heartbeat. We go through cycles and patterns recur, usually repeating themselves at the same level; we usually try to escape a reality that we do not appreciate so that we can move up the spiral. The structure of a spiral is always connected with time, space, matter and progression. Consequently, if we can discover the direction of that progression, we are able to enter into a state of attunement or resonance with the new reality, which makes our lives so much easier. In this state, there is also an important economy of energy, which can allow us to move on to a different level of being. This 'moving on' is no longer an indication of a 'movement towards' but rather the embrace of another level of being that encompasses the previous levels.

If you are swimming in a river, you can make for the

safety of the riverbank and maybe hurt yourself on hidden rocks; then you can go to the other bank, carried by the current. It is the matter of your body that moves in time and space. We can compare the riverbanks to the poles. However, if you stop moving from one riverbank to the other and just remain right in the middle of the river, you are carried along by it but you no longer have to resist the attraction of the matter of the banks. You may even dive right down to the riverbed where you will encounter a completely different reality, with fishes playing in and out of crevices among the stones while you travel at great speed unhindered by the rocks of the riverbanks. And then, following to the principle of neutralisation, there is the glory of the river merging with the sea. Where are you!

"A keen observation shows that the whole universe is a single mechanism working by the law of rhythm; the rise and fall of the waves, the ebb and flow of the tide, the waxing and waning of the moon, the sunrise and the sunset, the change of the seasons, the moving of the earth and of the planets, the whole cosmic system and the constitution of the entire universe are working under the law of rhythm. Cycles of rhythm, with major and minor cycles interpenetrating, uphold the whole creation in their swing. This demonstrates the origin of manifestation: that motion has sprung from the motionless life, and that every motion must necessarily result in a dual aspect. As soon as you move a stick, the single movement will make two points, the one where it starts and the other where it ends, the one strong and the other weak; to these a music conductor will count 'one, two,' 'one, two', a strong accent and a weak accent: one motion with two effects, each distinct and different from the other. It is this mystery that lies hidden under the dual aspect of all phases and forms of life; and the reason, cause, and significance of all life is found in rhythm."[19]

Movement is usually made towards or away from a particular form of manifestation, and this movement can be compared to the swing of a pendulum. Every action calls forth a reaction. There is always an advance and a retreat, an ebb and a flow, a rising and a falling, as there is with the chest when we breathe.

At the threshold of manifestation, vibration will be expressed as movements in a particular direction, towards a pole. The vibration, as it slowed down its movement became the universe at the moment of the Big Bang; thus was polarisation introduced, between then and now, a point of departure and the present moment. Poles are an outcome of the slowing down of vibration. A pole has been defined as one of two opposites, which form part of a system. It is a crystallisation of energy. A pole is established when and where the pendulum stops moving and then starts going in the opposite direction. At that point of apparent absence of movement, from that poised moment, and out of it, it seems that time and space, as well as form and organisation come into being. The fact that one pole cannot be created without its opposite immediately coming into being explains the duality of our universe and reality as we perceive it. The seed is planted in the matrix and an event then arises, the bearer of its own fruit and destruction, starting the joyous dance of order and dissolution, the play at one specific level on the stage of existence. But here, with the principle of rhythm, we are not concerned solely with the nature of the manifestations, whatever they may be, but with the movements inherent in these manifestations.

"The phenomenal world is always and everywhere in movement. All movement implies an energetic disequilibrium - no waterfall occurs without a difference in height, no electric current without two poles of different tensions, and so on...."[20]

Rhythm is life in motion, and the movement, as I have described, is always towards or away from a pole. The movement from one state to another, from one pole to another requires energy to sustain it and eventually that energy is spent. There would then appear to be a state of rest. However, the oscillation from one pole to the other, which appears to have come to an end, has in fact become so fine that it is no longer perceptible to our senses. This is the principle of neutralisation. In the apparent absence of movement, other levels of manifestation come into being. There seem to be successive states of manifestation ever finer, as the rates and modes of vibration increase. We can see this in life when people, who usually function from the head start aligning themselves with the prompting of their hearts. Forms of energy are then liberated from the confining influences of the grosser organisations and will be recognised, for example, in such qualities of the heart as intuition, courage, cordiality and attention. Every thought, emotion or mental state has its corresponding rate and mode of vibration, and therefore if the mind is still and there is attention, then the most sublime events occur and humans can express their creativity.

To illustrate this, let us just imagine that you have this wonderful toy, a sophisticated spinning top with holes in it, which you start pumping up and down. It emits a sound that increases in pitch as the pumping accelerates. After a time the sound becomes so high that you cannot hear it any more but then you notice that the top has started to heat up as the movement continues to increase. It will go through all the colours of the spectrum, from dull red to ultra violet and then it will start to disintegrate as the molecules disperse. The movement has become so fast that there would appear to be stillness. The faster the movement, the finer the manifestation. What appears to our senses to be the stillness of a level of manifestation seems to be the prerequisite for the movement from a finer, deeper level of manifestation, such as from sound to colour and from colour to light, for example. The poet T.S. Eliot describes this succinctly when he writes:

"At the still point of the turning world. Neither flesh nor fleshless;
Neither from nor towards; at the still point, there the dance is,
But neither arrest nor movement...." [21]

While this is true on the inner world, it also extends to the physical level. The body contains wonderful mechanisms which through the principle of rhythm enable it to achieve a state of balance naturally, economically and automatically. What are these elements that will help to determine physically the specific way in which our destiny may be eventually accomplished? It is hormones acting as messengers, which provide the increasingly refined system of communication that enables organs to function more and more subtly.

"It is now the opinion of leading biologists and students of genetics, such as Jennings, Davenport, Cunningham and others, that the theory of hereditary transmission through the determining influence of the chromosomes and genes must be abandoned and replaced by a newer, more scientific conception according to which it is not the chromosomes in the germ-cell, but hormones circulating in the maternal blood-stream during gestation, which fundamentally determine human heredity and destiny. In his work, 'Hormones and Heredity', Cunningham presents the theory that the transmission of hereditary traits is executed mostly through the influence of maternal hormones, and that the chromosomes are important only during the earliest period of development, prior to the appearance of the endocrine glands in the embryo. At this time, the work commenced by the chromosomes is taken over by the hormones. This theory has been accepted and extended by the American student of genetics, Davenport."[22]

Hormones are those mysterious, chemical messengers that maintain the balance in our being. To understand how they work, let us borrow the following description: "...think of the human body as a hotel switchboard, lit up by a constant stream of room-service orders and complaint calls: 'Can you lower the temperature in this room?' 'Would you send up a couple of cheeseburgers, please?' The mediators of this ceaseless biological babble - the messengers rushing from cell to cell to satisfy all requests - are powerful molecules called hormones. Named after the Greek word *hormon* (to set in motion), these ubiquitous chemical substances act, in ways still somewhat mysterious, to maintain the exquisite balance of being.

Even that doesn't begin to describe the frenzy of biochemical business going on in the human "hotel". Scientists who once thought hormones behaved like mere bell-hops now know they can sometimes act like manager, security guards, cleaning personnel - even guests - all talking to each other. That hormones govern every aspect of human experience from growth and development to reproduction, metabolism and moods has long been known. But researchers are just beginning to fathom the full range of what they do and how they work. 'The complex interactions in body function are absolutely astounding,' says Dr. Bert O'Malley, chairman of cell biology at Baylor College of Medicine and a former president of the Endocrine Society. 'Everything is kept in perfect balance by hormones not only for normal maintenance and survival but in response to anything that comes along - physical insult, mental stress, physical exertion, a thought process.'

New discoveries are constantly made about hormones. In an article *A Gland for all Seasons*,[23] the author Andrew Loudon discusses the following: "How long the day is influences everything from appetite to sex in many domestic and wild mammals. The pineal gland and its hormone, melatonin, may lie at the root of these seasonal changes in physiology and behaviour." While Andrew Scott, in *Messages in Evolution*, discusses how "human hormones are turning up in creatures as far removed from us as protozoa and plants. Perhaps our molecular messengers evolved from the chemical communications of primeval cells."[24]

"What is the hormonal system of the universe?" we may ask. Who are the messengers? What is the reality that lies behind the archetypal Hermes? Hasn't Hermes been called the "messenger of the gods", being a personification of the Egyptian god Thoth of earlier times who imparted to humanity the knowledge about the universal principles? These messengers, do they not appear to be the regulators of the rhythm of the universe in its movement of expansion and contraction? If there is a direction, then what is its goal and what is its meaning? Could it be that the meaning, the movement and the being of the universe are one and the same? When the poised energy, in suspension, finds its own direction of release and transformation, does it do so in accordance with a meaning which is its own being, its own glory?

An orderly system implies direction to the movement of the energy of that system. A human being is a specific system, with a specific purpose. Not only are we part of nature, enacting the cyclical purpose of being fruitful; but we are also conscious of our existence, which means that we can participate in the full realisation of our potential as human beings. "Potential can be either actualised or ignored, but it cannot be created or destroyed. All potential exists from the beginning and is eternal, as is the One whose being contains and sustains it."[25] One of the purposes of the body of humanity, and therefore of all the cells that constitute it, is to actualise consciousness of consciousness, to achieve the full realisation that we know that we know and to put that knowledge in practice. As with the seed, which will die and be discarded if the purpose that is the plant is not realised, so the cells die as we do in the process. If the purpose of the seed is accomplished, it finds a new glory in the plant that goes on to produce thousands of seeds. Try however to explain the plant to the seed! In its limited "consciousness", it will have no notion of what you are talking about. And so, in the same way, we humans, shy away from the abstraction of this awareness and tend to dismiss it. We forget that as the custodians of this extraordinary gift of self reflection, we possess a key to the door that can open and reveal to us the understanding of our true nature. The principle of rhythm leads us in measured motion to this key that is the heart. Such a movement of energy can only happen when there is a fine attention and complete, spontaneous silence at the level of thought and mind. In the silence of the heart, where neither lover nor beloved exists any longer, what is the dawn, whose shining light awakens the lights within the trillions of cells, and annihilates you? The seed transformed is the plant; the seed exists no longer.

The heart is able to know meaning of which the thought processes know nothing. The principle of rhythm can however be seen at work in both mental and physical spheres; as thought processes are mechanical in nature and need energy to sustain them, so they will seek to control their own supply of the living energy of the human being, using fear in order to maintain the *status quo*, fighting against both meaning and transformation. (If a person changes, energy may no longer be available to the thought processes, producing insecurity and fear.)

All too often, when a problem or a difficulty arises in our life, we burn up our energy in fruitless anxiety and attempts to find a solution. We may even try to manipulate a problem by "positive thinking", prayer or concentration on it. In fact, all these activities merely ensure that the problem continues to exist on the same level, maybe disappearing for a while, only to reappear later with greater intensity.

There is a different approach. When there is awareness of a fact, with no thought processes attempting to suppress or express the energy of that fact, the energy seems for a while to be poised, and in that state of suspension, something new is created. The energy starts moving of its own accord. Movement is a progression in a particular direction. Then the energy of the fact evolves its own direction of release, of transformation. Order is therefore created at a different level from the one at which the energy was originally operating. This movement is spontaneous and, most of the time, unconscious at the level at which the energy of the fact is used. It is operating in accordance with its own necessity, with no effort because we are now in the domain of unity. There is a single energy and a dance of forms issuing from it. In transformation, the release is naturally from the lesser to the greater, from complexity to simplicity in as much as the energy of the fact is always working to express its highest potential. In paradise revisited, the order of one level – the heart level for example – may well be the disorder of another grosser level such as the one on which thought processes operate.

Rhythm is hidden at the root of every activity, be it constructive or destructive, and the outcome of every activity depends on its rhythm. The bird moves its wings rhythmically to fly, and it is the same rhythmic contraction and expansion that causes the fish to swim and the snake to glide. As rhythm is innate in humans and works to maintain their health, so in the same way everything in their lives depends on it; success or failure, right action and wrong action, are all accounted for in some way or other by a change of rhythm. It plays just as important a role in the mind as in the body; the transition from joy to sorrow, the coming and going of different thoughts, and the whole way in which our minds work involve rhythm, and all confusion and despair would seem to be the result of a lack of rhythm in the mind.

"Rhythm in every guise, be it called game, play, amusement, poetry, music or dance, is the very nature of man's whole constitution. When the entire mechanism of his body is working in a rhythm, the beat of the pulse, of the heart, of the head, the circulation of the blood, hunger and thirst, all show rhythm, and it is the breaking of rhythm that is called disease. When the child is crying and the mother does not know what ails it, she holds it in her arms and pats it on the back. This sets the circulation of the blood, the pulsations and the whole mechanism of the body in rhythm; in other words sets the body in order, and soothes the child. The nursery rhyme 'Pat-a-cake', which is known all the world over in some form or other, cures a child of fretfulness by setting its whole being in rhythm. Therefore physicians depend more upon the examination of the pulse than on anything else in discovering the true nature of disease, together with the examination of the beat of the heart and the movement of the lungs in the chest and back."[26]

It is through rhythm that our emotional nature can be awakened, be it through dance, singing or poetry. The heart can then start to express meaning through intuition, in an immediate response to the necessity of the moment, a fulfilment of our natural way of being. As the refinement of the frequency of our vibrations becomes greater, we can start to experience a reality at levels of perception that are not usual for us, levels that are much more deeply grounded in other dimensions with different energies from those we use in our everyday lives. We can return to T.S. Eliot, and say with him:

"... Except for the point, the still point
There would be no dance, and there is only the dance."

It is at that still point that our energies may be poised ready for expression or manifestation. Intuition then replaces instinct and there is a leap into creativity. It is also the domain where transformation can take place.

There are two types of intuition. There is the one that arises from sublimated knowledge, and which is still related to thought processes and memory. It always contains an element of doubt. And there is the other one which is the intuition of the heart with the quality of tremendous energy and creative action which the other does not possess. In other words, if intuition is not accompanied by the burning necessity to act, it is wiser to wait and question its lack of dynamism. Very often one would find that the energy has been used to bring up to the surface forgotten knowledge. When we act with the intuition that is the outcome of a pure movement of the heart, we often find that what is required has already taken place or is in the process of completion.

Intuition is the partner of inspiration and the rhythmic undercurrent between them propels you through different dimensions that lend their music to the harmony which is being created. The ultimate work of art that we are stems from the harmonisation of the masculine and feminine aspects of our being discussed in chapter 1 which is subject to the principle of gender with which the principle of rhythm has an affinity. The balance in the subtle vibrations between intuition and inspiration will inform and nourish both our feminine and our masculine aspects. Once the less dominant aspect starts to express itself without however negating the other aspect, the oscillation between these two parts of a person's nature becomes more rapid, hence finer and a state of harmony ensues. That person will then act in harmony with whichever aspect is appropriate or necessary in any given situation, without negating the other aspect.

If we consider the creation of a human being, the energy that precipitates at conception is a vibration that slows down in order to incarnate. In vibration, there are always two activities present, one of contraction and one of expansion. (See chapter 6 - The principle of vibration). As rhythm is life disguised in motion, which is always towards or away from a pole, and as the underlying pattern is the actualisation of our potential, then in that context contraction will therefore mean "moving away from" and expansion will mean "moving towards". These two tendencies will be reflected in two abilities and two aspects: in the ability to perceive in awareness and the masculine aspect, and in the ability to respond to what we are aware of and the feminine aspect.

The first tendency is established during the first four-and-a-half months of our gestation, while the second one is established during the last four-and-a-half months. We are these two patterns, with one usually being dominant and the other secondary. Most of the time our lives are lived from the standpoint of only one of these patterns. Consider a couple who are having supper when their baby starts crying in the bedroom. The father will say that the baby is crying whereas the mother is already half-way to the door. The father's dominant pattern is that of perception with response as the secondary one; the mother's dominant pattern is of response. Though it must be noted that this conditioning is at last changing, through listening to the rhythmic waves of development which were present during our own gestation period, we can infer the rhythms which have been operating since our birth and thus enter into resonance with the primal rhythms of creation.

In the evolution of a life, a young baby functions very much at the level of animal instincts with a diffuse type of consciousness that will provide the behavioural pattern of undifferentiated monism. "I am you". The ego boundaries are not yet established as the personality develops. In terms of consciousness we can say that the child will perceive patterns without necessarily questioning their meaning or attempting to give a direction to their energies. A quest for meaning comes with puberty and adolescence when the quality or state of being of a person is asserted and social interaction starts in earnest. From that time on, the response to the patterns of which we are conscious is established. If only one of these two abilities is cultivated at the expense of the other, and we are perceiving without response, or responding without being aware of what we are responding to, there will be a state of unbalance. Pathologically, the extreme manifestation of the first occurrence is autism, the second is present in the Down's syndrome.

The play is between two poles: perception with awareness and response without a person sending the pendulum wildly swinging to one pole or the other. Again, the key to the harmonisation of these tendencies: to perceive in awareness and to respond, is to be found in the heart and more precisely in the principle of neutralisation in rhythm. As the oscillation becomes finer, the poles get closer; the two "absences" blend and in the void which is created, there is the possibility of a leap in a subtler dimension of being.

Apart from the factor of love, which is beyond the

swing of the pendulum, all our actions will call forth a reaction. We may at times be concerned with the law of cause and effect in our every day life, trying to explain what happens to us through that law; at times it may be wiser to stand back and observe that, like pendulums, we are just swinging from one state to another.

What does it mean 'to stand back'? Two attributes of objective love are spontaneity and lack of identification. These prevent the ego from appropriating the energy of the facts that crowd our daily life, whether inwardly or outwardly. Sound asleep, would you be able to say: 'I sleep'? 'I', being a form of the mind does not exist in deep sleep. What hears but the ears! What sees but the eyes! The ego likes to monopolise the energy.

A simple exercise, derived from a sentence uttered by Einstein, can circumvent the ego's appetite for control and power. The most important word in the French language is the word 'il' from the phrase "il y a" which means 'there is'. Using this exercise one says that there is tiredness, not that I am tired, that there is joy, or grief, not that I am joyous, or in grief, that there is a headache, not that I have a headache, and so on. In this way we do not emphasise one state of affairs as opposed to another, good health as opposed to sickness for example, because we know that when we emphasise a positive, we are at the same time creating a negative state. The facts are recognised for what they are, without their energies feeding the ego's appetite. Facts are truths expressed at the level of the awareness with which we are functioning. Truths contain tremendous power which is constantly seeking to release itself. The energy which is freed accelerates the oscillation of the pendulum from one state to another. Joy, pain, grief, tiredness, a headache, are all manifestations of energy which is valid at the level at which they occur. Through love that lets be and the rhythm inherent in all manifestations of life, there can be an alteration of subconscious predisposition and unconscious conditioning which frees the energies that can transform the patterns of our existence.

Love also allows the principle of neutralisation to come into effect in our relationships. As the oscillation between one state and another becomes finer, we cannot help but recognise that everything is everything. Our interdependence with one another, with the earth and the cosmos is now increasingly acknowledged. Furthermore, we begin to recognise that we are all of the same fabric, whether we are English or African, Russian or Chilean; when we need to eat we all feel the same pangs of hunger. If I want to help you, I must be honest and ask myself: what is it that I lack? When we notice a need in someone, then we must ask what is it that we ourselves lack and attend to that. The intensity of being that is generated in us when we truly attend to our own needs, produces an energy that helps create a situation in which others can take from us what is necessary, just as the roots of a plant take from the earth the nourishment they need. It is not the earth that gives, it is the roots that take.

"There is no important difference between live and dead matter, since both are made up of live entities"[27]. "Since the universe is nothing but live beings, each controlling his own level and his own relationships, there is absolutely nothing in the universe that needs to be corrected in any way. We don't have to do anything about it, whatever it is. There is consciousness everywhere in the universe, and we can trust all beings to handle their own decisions. No matter how it looks to us, love never loses control: the laws of our relations are as honest and exact as the laws of physics".[28]

Summary

We can see rhythm everywhere: in the tides, the seasons, the breath and the orbits of the planets. Even in human affairs we usually notice the fall of that which rises; the departure of that which arrives.

Rhythmic movement is oscillation between two poles: the movement towards a pole, the instant of arrival, the return towards the other pole.

A harmonious, orderly, purposeful system is in balance: its movements appear regulated, poised, and dynamic. A system in disequilibrium may lurch violently from one pole to another. The elements that maintain rhythmic equilibrium - hormones in the body, for example - are themselves complex "messengers".

Rhythm underlies health and disease, success and failure. Attention to the pulse - of the body, of dance, of music, of nature - can restore failing equilibrium.

In some circumstances, rhythmic movement appears to become very fine, fluid, subtle, and harmonious. For example, an individual who is fully at ease with the masculine and feminine elements of their psyche may move rapidly from one to the other in an effortless, seamless flow. Here, a principle of "neutralisation" appears. The oscillations become so fine and rapid that they in effect produce a new state of being. The poles lose their polarity. A transformation occurs, a different state arises, an old pattern dies, a new creation manifests.

In daily life we may experience this as "moving on" instead of "moving to and fro".

CHAPTER FIVE

"To be or not to be - that is the question" or rather to be and not to be, paradoxical unity

Embrace the facts and leap into unity

Apole can be defined as each of the extremities of the axis of a sphere or, figuratively, as each of the two opposed principles to which parts of a system are referable. Simply observing the world around us, we see that there are two extremes, or poles to every state. There is day and night, light and darkness, heat and cold, nadir and zenith, sharp and blunt, joy and sadness, and so on.

These extremes of manifestation embody a force with a specific dynamism through which the principle of polarity works. We usually see polarity as being an attraction towards a particular object, or a tendency or trend in a specific direction. Polarity is also understood to be the particular attitude of mind of a person, expressed, for example, in a propensity towards either awareness or responsiveness, towards the male or the female, individuality or sociability, detachment or identification. Currently, this principle can also be understood in present society as meaning a sense of balance in attitudes of mind and normality of outlook.

The principle of polarity states that all is duality. Everything has poles, everything has its pair of opposites. In nature, we have the sun and the moon, with their masculine and feminine aspects of projection and reflection, fire and water, earth and air, birth and death. Everything and every being need these opposite qualities in order to exist, to act and to fulfil their purpose in life; for each quality is incomplete without the other.

We see this principle of polarity at work in all things and in all beings, in the two sides of the body, for example, and in the head and the feet. The right brain and the left brain are another example with the left brain, the source of logical and rational thought, enabling us to talk and read, to reason deductively, to remember detail, and to measure time, while the right brain is the originator of ideas, of spatial sense, intuition, music, emotion, and an awareness of the timeless, the spaceless and the formless. Neither side is better than the other.

I was talking to a woman who had been doing T'ai chi for two years and she told me that she had realised that the right side of her body was really extending into the movement, going right into it with the energy flowing. She connected this with the masculine, left side of her brain. But she then realised that when she did the same movements on the left side of the body, she went only a half or a quarter as far, though she felt that she was going the whole way. Noticing the difference meant that she felt she had to work very hard on the feminine aspect of her being. By deciding to do so, she was in fact using the already over-active left side of her brain, connected with the masculine aspect, to try and achieve balance. She was denying the importance of the function of the opposite pole, of the right hemisphere of her brain. Was there another way to achieve balance? The simple realisation that, while doing the exercise, she was stopping the complete extension of the movements with the left side, the very acknowledgement of the fact and letting it be, would create a matrix wherein which the energy of the whole brain could start working in earnest. It is the left side of the brain that gives importance to the separation between the two hemispheres but we should remember that the brain is one entity and that there is communication going on all the time between both parts. In the matrix of attention and power, which is truly a matrix of love, the energy of the whole brain could then take over and establish the balance between the two sides - integration. The masculine side would no longer be urging the other, feminine side to extend more into the movement of the exercise. It would happen spontaneously and without effort as the energy would work of its own accord. It did, bringing about what was right for that person.

The principle of polarity is expressed not only in the human body but also in our relationships. The most beautiful illustration of opposing qualities at work is to be found in the fulfilment of life, the conception in love of a child. The keen attentiveness of the two partners to one another circumvents sexuality – which is a distortion that the mind has created in order to keep control over the extraordinary energy of sex – and then the sexual act is no longer just an act of physical release. Through attention comes the perception of the actual magnetism involved, the sexual magnetism, which is like electricity with its opposing poles. The receptive pole is the female sexual organ and the active pole is the male sexual organ. There is the purely animal function of the two poles meeting when heat is produced and there is sexual release. If we consider another level however, the active and positive pole of the male organ and man's lower part of the body is complemented by a negative pole, which is the upper part of his body. With a woman, the vagina and the lower part of her body constitute the negative and receptive pole, while the upper part of the body is the positive pole. When two partners meet with their own individual polarity truly balanced, whether in a heterosexual or a homosexual embrace, then they may experience an orgasm that have very little to do with a mere release of energy. Through the attention of the partners to one another, an awakening occurs within each one as the poles merge.

For the heterosexual couple, the man will activate the positive pole in the woman, which then triggers in her a current of energy between the sexual organs and the upper part of her body. And as the woman does the same for the man, attentive through intuition, so the man's body begins to vibrate in its own polarity, and the two partners truly join in the glory of the celebration of their human beingness. For homosexuals, active and passive partners will find in one another the same type of completion. The celibate may taste directly, without external help, the experience of mystical union. There is a feeling of timelessness, a forgetting of the space one occupies, and an absence of the notion of who one is, something that is noticed only afterwards, when one comes out of the state of communion. This type of attention is a mark of great love. There is sex at the level of simple physical relief; but there is also sex when, through love, attention may come into play allowing the awakening of the polarity of the two partners or directly within oneself. There is the unification of both male and female qualities as well as of the masculine and feminine within each partner, which is the essence of true union.

The relationship between the poles within each partner is one of balance and completion of each other. As partners meet, these forces exercise an attraction upon one another. Like attracts or awakens like through its opposite pole, or is always recognised by like. Besides this attraction of like to like in terms of polarity, there is the attraction of each to its opposite as with heterosexual partners.

Existing, as we do, in the domain of time, space and matter, we see duality everywhere. But apparently opposite qualities are only the two extremes of the same thing, with many varying degrees in between. An oscillating pendulum will move from one pole to the other. The momentum towards one pole will cease and the gravitational pull will draw it towards the opposite pole. The greater the impulse towards one pole, the greater will be the impulse to the other pole. In this way, one pole creates the other. There will however be a gradual loss of energy in the movement from one pole to the other.

By extension, we can say that through the principle of polarity human beings attract and create their own reality. The one pole of our reality is in harmony with the level of consciousness – the other pole - on which we live our life. Everything around us and in us is in a continual state of resonance with the vibrational rate of energy at which we choose to function. Our own magnetic field creates or draws to us, every second of the day, the perfect inner or outer event. Everything is therefore perfect and cannot be otherwise as our reality is in harmony with our level of consciousness.

The two poles are connected, with a range of expression between them. If we are dissatisfied with our reality and want to change it, we need to change our level of consciousness. Otherwise we go on repeating the same patterns. I was shown one clear example of these repeated patterns when a lady, just returned from her honeymoon, in great distress told me that her new husband was as cruel as her previous two husbands. And she wondered why she had not seen it before. Her search for material security had in fact prevented her from being aware of the pattern of victimisation that she projected, thereby attracting cruelty.

Each aspect of ourselves – body, mind, emotion, behaviour – makes a vibrational contribution to our whole consciousness, and we will attract and start responding to corresponding vibrations in others. In other words, our responses to the outside world are the reflection of those responses to our inner world. If, in our environment, we cannot find the same vibrations that we need to evolve, we will start creating that reality for ourselves. We will move house, town or country, driven as it were by a home sickness that we had not previously known. We always have the experiences and perceptions appropriate to our level of vibration.

If we feel dense and miserable, a cluster of events will arise, seemingly at random, which affirm and prolong that inner state and prevent energies of a more vibrant nature from reaching us. If, however, we become aware of that state, open to it and let it be, then there is a movement of expansion, which will allow finer vibrations to enter, and we will find ourselves being carried to a healthier state through the energy of that movement.

A lady, who looked as if she was in her late middle-age, had visited different physiotherapists and osteopaths over many years seeking relief from the back pain, which she had endured since falling from a horse in her early twenties. No one had been able to find the source of her pain and in spite of it she had stopped taking pain killers because of their side effects. After we had discussed the problem, she came to understand that the power of simply acknowledging the fact is sufficient to release the fact from within and she also realised how important it was to stop giving energy to her search for pain relief. Her mind was slightly more at rest when she left to go and meet a friend who happened to tell her of the wonderful treatment he had just received from a chiropractor who had recently arrived in London from the United States. A fortnight later, I met her and mistook her for her own daughter. Her pain had gone following treatments from this new chiropractor, and so had the numerous wrinkles on her face. A new vibrancy was shining through.

By attending to the facts and letting them be there is a change in our level of awareness and we start to attract a new reality. When we fall in love, then everything around us and everything in us takes on a different hue. We sing to the stars. We are consumed by a passion hitherto unknown. We make eternal vows. Reality is coloured with the brush of our subjectivity. The pain, when we fall out of love, will be equal to the energy invested in the relationship. When our vibrations change, the whole world looks different. I myself experienced this in a most wondrous fashion some years ago when I came to realise that, for various reasons, I was doing what I felt obliged to do as opposed to what I knew was right for me. By simply acknowledging this fact, a shift in my consciousness provoked a wonderful transformation in my life.

If we don't like our reality, then we will attempt to change it. And the only way in which we can do this is by raising our vibrational level, expression of our consciousness. But how can we change our level of awareness? What are the factors that can change one level and bring the manifestations of that level to another? What makes ice change to water?

Love is the all-consuming energy that will destroy a level of organisation and free its restrictive structures in order to establish another more life-encompassing level. Love knows nothing of morality and judgement, personality and personal history, cause and effect, or duality.

"Start by loving your negative feelings, your own boredom, dullness and despair. It's hard to believe, but changing the *content* of your mind does nothing to change your vibration level. For the purpose of raising your awareness, it is useless to change your ideas, your faith, your behavior, your place of residence, or your companions. It is not arbitrary nor an accident that you are where you are, so you might as well get your attitude straight before you make a change. Otherwise you might find yourself chasing all over creation looking for the right place, and not even the Sea of Infinite Bliss will feel right to you."[29]

In an American town where I was lecturing, my hostess mentioned that her neighbour had asked to see me. She had had a successful career in industry after marrying quite a few times, and I was informed that her vanity had been served by her great wealth. Recently she had experienced a conversion and belonged now to a "born-again Christian" sect to which she was devoting her life, caring for the poor, having disposed of all her business interests. A middle-aged lady came in. I overheard her draw my hostess's attention to the little blouse that she had just bought at the Salvation Army and for which she had paid only .25 cents. After all those changes in her life, her vanity was still present.

What does it mean to be loving? The only way we can identify it is through facts, through feelings, emotions, physical and psychological pains, knowledge, drive, how we relate to the rest of the world and to ourselves, and so on. And nothing is secret because our energy field is like a parchment on which everything of importance is written, everything that has ever been and everything that is. This is why we can be read like an open book. Ask any medium or clairvoyant to tell you how they proceed.

Without comment or judgement, without comparing or desire, if we are attentive to all these facts that we are and to what we are beyond them, and if we agree to let these facts be, simply respecting the energies that they manifest, respecting their very being, only then there arises a subtle type of communication, of these facts and the whole of ourselves, a communication which includes dimensions that the mind cannot fathom. We experience a tremendous love at work that directs the reality of our life towards the need for realisation of our being. We are free and self-determined beings, regardless of how we limit our awareness, through mental handicap, depression or apathy. If we acknowledge this, we can all relax, for we know that no individual or group of beings can control our vibration level. And this is why no-one can be abandoned or forgotten. There is nothing in the universe, especially in the physical part of it, that can counter our free will to love and to love again.

If we ruin and destroy, maim and murder, we are practising self-mutilation because on the battlefield of love we are all one body. Celebrate the foot that treads lightly on this one earth which the runner in friendly competition with you uses as the basis for her excellence just as you do. With lightness of heart recognise the lightness of being of others, who are yourself, for there are no "others" in the democracy of love.

We use violent confrontation with our selves to perpetuate the victim syndrome and to remain losers. But if we are not happy with the present state of affairs in which we find ourselves and want to change it, then it is important to change the level of awareness that equates to the vibration at which we function. However, a good deal of energy is required to change level. Usually, we seek outside ourselves and try to accumulate energy through different religious practices, through exercises, diet, and other such pursuits. Acting in this way according to previous experience we are simply adding more fuel to the actual state of affairs and do not transform. If we continue to base our action on the experience of one level, then we remain in a straitjacket, a vicious circle, only exploring within the spectrum of the vibrations which pertain to that level. It becomes obvious that only by changing the frequency of our vibration will we attract a new reality. Why not be winners and consider the power and the glory of the facts that we are instead of trying to avoid them, and love the very characteristics that we want to change by acknowledging them and letting them be. These characteristics will then free their energy and a new vibrational level will occur, with a new consciousness and a different reality.

Through observation, we cannot help but notice that there are forces at work in the universe and in ourselves which balance and complete each other. Within the context of matter, time and space, movement is always occurring between two pauses, or seems to be going from one rest to another rest, from one absence to another. When we breathe, we stop inhaling so that we can exhale and vice-versa. The reason we notice rests or pauses or absences of movement is that we consider events within the context of duality, which is illusion because the two poles are "made up" of absences. We persist in our limited perception of reality and the limitations of our subjective consciousness continue to produce the positive and the negative, the expressive and the responsive, the cycles of destruction and creation, of life and of death. We perceive only our own level of consciousness.

This perception also affects the direction in which our thoughts go. Direction implies meaning, and with the mind we also have direction towards a pause or a rest. If however on reaching the pause attention is keen, then a state of suspension may occur and meanings of other dimensions of being can be felt. In this state of suspension, intimations of eternity and infinity can arise, "understood", as it were from the standpoint of the unmanifest, the limitless, the timeless and the spaceless. Only a deep underlying love, without object, can reveal these dimensions because it is in the heart that many answers are found. Poetry and mysticism, previously regarded by many as arbitrary and as describing only a subjective reality, have been hinting at meanings that are now beginning to be discussed and verified by scientists. Science makes us face the void. In his articles Dr. David Bohm describes a holographic universe and new discoveries in quantum physics have ushered in global interaction creating a world in an eternal state of interconnection. There is no separation in the quantum universe.

Krishnamurti spoke of "the corridor of opposites" that people usually walk up and down, swinging from love to hate, from confidence to anxiety, from peace to war. These are the poles that set the limits of our daily experience and of the general behaviour of society. If there is to be a deep change, there must be a movement outside this corridor, which is something that may happen when the principle of polarity is thoroughly understood and the mind is no longer preoccupied with these "opposites". There is then a form of contact with the unmanifest that truly leads to a change of perception. We travel from the domain of time, space and matter towards the abstract, going from form to formlessness. The void at last! The void instructs plenitude of its grandeur, and plenitude invites a greater void whose dynamic action opens the door to nothingness. The mystics of the past knew its threshold, the very threshold at which matter, as energy and consciousness, places us now.

The action of the principle of polarity is the portal through which the unmanifest becomes manifest. It is as if the central light of the unmanifest, expressed through finer and higher principles, divides existence into two forms, light and darkness. Then the puzzle of duality begins, the idea of opposites keeping us trapped in illusion. But darkness is only less light compared with more light.

There are two ways at our immediate disposal of overriding these deceptive types of organisation: the sliding way and the monkey way, as we may find in the Kybalion.

Where indeed does darkness "end" and light "begin"? Every manifestation of life is expressing polarity, which we tend to classify as either positive or negative. These poles are simply manifestations of varying degrees of vibration. If, once the principle of polarity is grasped, we want to bring about change, then it is simply a question of sliding along the scale of vibration from one pole towards the other. This way entails effort and application. An example of the sliding way can be seen in the case of a person who is jealous and becomes aware that this jealousy is creating havoc in her relationships. Through counselling or effort of will, or maybe psychoanalysis, the person comes to understand the deep underlying patterns of her behaviour and eventually manages to keep the emotion in check.

The monkey way, however, is the way of objective love. There is the fact of jealousy, which is the exact expression of desire and possessiveness on a specific level of awareness. By attention to the facts of the desire and of the need to possess equate to jealousy, and by letting that fact be, without looking for the cause, without judgement or attempting to change anything, energy is at the disposal of the monkey that you are. This energy enables you to catch hold of an upper branch and you witness the oscillation of the pendulum from jealousy to its opposite pole which appears on the horizon. Spontaneously, there is generosity. Transformation is being brought about by the very energy of the wonderful fact of jealousy. And without effort. The energy thus freed helps the monkey to go on up to a yet higher branch. There is generosity; that is the fact. The pendulum swings again to another pole, that of abundance, and from abundance to loving care and so it goes on. Life is always working toward the realisation of the highest potential that was already at the heart of the fact of jealousy.

It is important to simply notice facts, and acknowledge their presence, letting them be and even letting go of the knowledge, rather than giving importance to a positive state, because in this latter instance we are creating a negative state at the same time and we must accept our responsibility for doing so. Any ideal, be it of well-being, peace, love, beauty or goodness is always accompanied by its opposite. Mother Teresa is reported as saying: "Jesus never said: 'Love Humanity'; he said: 'Love your neighbour as you love yourself'. " The neighbour is a fact, the love of humanity is an ideal. An ideal of peace will actively create war. The pursuit of happiness is self-defeating. The energy of the living present is used to confirm, to compare, to analyse and to dissect and this is always done with reference to the past, something dead, and this does not transform the unhappiness; the energy is being used in the pursuit, not in the creation of happiness. Resistance to something gives it life, non-resistance lets it burn itself out. The one-sided person will have no balance. As balance is an aspect of nature, by just allowing whatever is to be, nature will gain control and restore that balance. It is the security of life.

Imagine a boulder in the middle of a river, brought there by a force of the water which is itself interacting with the configuration of the river banks. The water has to flow around it. One's inclination might well be to move the boulder, so that the river can flow unimpeded. Considering the boulder to be in the wrong place is simply a consequence of the way our minds work. The rock is a manifestation of energy as is the river as is the disturbance. In a field of boulders our boulder would simply not be noticed. We could compare the boulder to a disease in the body. The reason we have such difficulty in understanding transformation is because it operates through a dissolution of the patterns and structures of an organisation, a disease, as well as of the system, the body, where it is found. Energy is freed that allows another level to be established where system and organisation are unified, the disease having disappeared in the movement which is faster than the speed of light. The manifestation and its system "visit" therefore the dimension of the formless, the spaceless and the timeless. Then there is transformation.

There are many levels of manifestations of energy interpenetrating one another that we can see. In therapies, for example, when the practitioner tries to get rid of a disease and promote the well-being of a person, he is usually attempting to induce a state of affairs in which one manifestation is destroyed so that there is a uniform flow of energy through the whole person. The usual approach is to manipulate the manifestation. However, unless the inherent purpose of that manifestation is fulfilled, it will reappear later on. As soon as there is a conscious effort to move in any particular direction, the deep movement of transcendence is blocked.

Our responses to the outside world are the reflection of

the responses to our inner world. If we acknowledge that a fact is a fact and see it as such, then we know that there is no sense in trying to avoid a particular situation or to contrive a change in it. For, the more we contrive or avoid, the less likely we are to make any meaningful change. If the mind is at peace, there is no direction given to the energy of the situation or of the fact. Indeed a state of resonance arises. The energy of the state or of the fact, when it is not directed by the limited mind, is able to find its own way of release or transformation.

Hamlet's question "To be or not to be?", plenitude or void? must be asked again but now we have come to the paradoxical unity[30] of the question: to be and not to be. Can we embrace both states in consciousness? As the laws that regulate nature teach us, everything interpenetrates everything else and in the end reaches equilibrium, the hidden is revealed, and what dies is reborn at another level. In the continuous alternation of void and plenitude, destruction and creation, we are led to ever deeper realisations.

Let us imagine a sphere whose periphery is infinitely elastic. It encloses a multitudes of spheres encased one in the other. Our sphere is itself contained within spheres upon spheres. The wall of our sphere is composed of smaller spheres whose walls in their turn are made up of yet more smaller spheres and so on. Each sphere is in a continuous movement of contraction and expansion and has the ability to change its orbit and its direction as it hurtles throughout the space that its movement creates. Let us now consider each point on the wall of a sphere;

one point cannot exist without being in opposition to another point. The two opposite points are called poles and the relationship between them illustrates the principle of polarity at work.

The spheres may represent the whole of reality as we perceive it, or the cosmos, or the cells of the human body itself with all its layers of luminosity. And now for the ultimate act of imagination: in a silent state of suspension, spheres come into alignment, worlds within worlds file past and you are propelled into the dimension from which they constantly arise, out of time, space and form, into unity. The smile, then, oh, the smile...

"Eons ago, before there was physical matter, you were one with us. Your essence remains, even now, indistinguishable from the unified field of being out of which flow duality, multiplicity, and all that flourishes in the eternal play of polarities. In oneness with the Eternal Source, in flowing, fluid realms of all-spectrum light and love, we lived together in the early ages of the morning. Together we shared a common "I." As waves of energy, we flowed through fields of dreams, the landscape of our eternal home."[31]

We called a movement from one pole to its opposite the principle of rhythm (see previous chapter) and the two points themselves the manifestation of the force which we call the principle of polarity. We have seen that the two extremes towards which the pendulum oscillates are the poles. There the movement stops, to start again in the opposite direction. As everything that exists does so within the domain of polarity, then everything is absence of movement, everything is 'maya' or illusion. Is there an underlying factor as the basis of reality? The movement of contraction and expansion at the origin of the poles is called the principle of vibration.

SUMMARY

Nature shows us that everything has two aspects: day and night, heat and cold, nadir and zenith. Two opposite points are called poles; the dynamic tension between them is polarity.

We see the principle of polarity in human life as well: the masculine and the feminine, conflict and harmony, good and bad. One pole cannot, ever, exist without the other.

We frequently attempt to enjoy only the good, the "nice" side of a polarity. We want the fun, the affection, the life. We want never to experience the depression, the arguments, the death.

Yet it is an impossible task to separate the two. More often than not, if we try to cling to calm affection we get incessant squabbling. Becoming obsessive about health we fall ill. We may appear to be stuck in a "corridor of opposites". As we avoid our shadow it becomes darker and more powerful. It grips us more tightly.

The strange paradox is that if we embrace one pole, the other may appear on the horizon of our consciousness. We do not, then, waste energy in the hopeless attempt to shut out the truth. Instead, that energy is a force for liberation, for movement to a higher standpoint where we are no longer locked in the corridor at all.

CHAPTER SIX

THE
PRINCIPLE
OF
VIBRATION

Vibration – midway between the roar of creation and the whimper of the big bang

Scientific discoveries have revealed that the universe is in a constant state of evolution, an ongoing gestation, the origin of which, 15 billion years or so ago with the Big Bang, was the blue print of the paradigm shift that the consciousness of humanity is now undergoing at another level of the spiral. The human race was the last species to appear on Earth. It will be the first to go as it embraces its light inheritance.

The mirror image is always presenting the reverse of what it reflects. Then, the Big Bang saw the passage of the non-manifest to the manifest, that is the creation of the universe which is subject to the laws deriving from the principles that regulate its appearance in time, space and matter, - the laws of gender, causation, correspondence, rhythm and polarity.

There is today a consensus, that a finer type of consciousness is emerging, a consciousness that I myself have experienced. The mystics and saints described their experiences of something of that nature at an individual level but now there is developing a greater interest in, and understanding of such matters in society generally. This leads us to realise that we are also regulated by principles which operate out of time, space and matter. The mind has to bring itself to embrace the uncertainty that this entails as this is a level that it cannot control; the laws deriving from these principles are those of vibration, creative   impulse,   insight/illumination   and communication/communion. The paradigm shift is from dualism to holism, from idealism to the actuality of the fact, from conventional to atomic warfare, from the periphery to the nucleus, from God out there or within, to the One.

The universe is constantly recreating itself through metamorphosis, which indicates the direction of its evolution. In order to participate in that process and to consciously integrate these transformations, we cannot attach ourselves to any manifestation of the life force. Instead, by embracing them, they can become springboards from which we can dive into the dimensions of being that we are first and foremost, unmanifest, out of space, time and form, from which who we are derives. Try and imagine the sun leaping in pure joy into the light beyond the light that it is.

In our pursuit of the study of the universal principles, we are now entering a domain where exploration is conducted more on the level of intuitive insight than that of the mind. Belonging, as it does, to the realm of matter, time and space, it is only with great difficulty that the mind will fathom these more rarefied domains of the timeless, spaceless and formless.

We are hardly in a position to comprehend directly the nature of the consciousness that generates the thought that creates the cosmos, given that before substance comes into being, there is no time or space, no mind or form. However, through analogy, we can attempt to gain an insight into that dimension. Generally, for activity to be set in motion, three factors are necessary: a purpose, a thought and a design, the design being created in accordance with the thought that helps realise the purpose. For example, the purpose of creating a chair is to have a piece of furniture on which one can sit comfortably. This will be thought out by a designer who will then draw up the design. These three stages exist in the abstract as far as the chair is concerned; the project will start to materialise when the wood is cut according to the design. The design stage exists nearer materialisation than the thought of the designer does. If, for example, there is a mistake in the design, it will be much more laborious to make changes at the drawing board than if a mistake had occurred at the thinking stage, because the design is closer to actualisation in matter than the idea is.

For our purposes, the principle of vibration can be compared to the design stage, the principle of creative impulse which we will consider in the next chapter representing the conception of the design. So everything begins with what we understand to be a thought. Thought focuses. This focus of thought as an abstract form calls forth energy and energy generates substance. The purpose or motive behind the thought gave form to the creation of the cosmos, for example. But its reason for being, and its very being, are one and the same. One of the meanings of the word 'cosmos' is 'order'. Order is laws applied in accordance with a specific direction.

A womb is necessary in order for a new human being to develop physically. We can compare the design stage to a matrix that has been "formed" outside time, space and matter by the light of some transcendental dynamic *deus ex machina,* – at the level of the "idea" or the thinking stage, – that will observe itself developing, for example, as the elementary consciousness of the sperm and the ovum to the fully-fledged consciousness of the human being. There are two aspects to our being, one inside time, space and matter, the other outside them. These two aspects are contained in, and evolve from, a greater matrix, that of the level of the purpose, beyond time, space and matter, that is the very impulse of life and intelligence whose action is creation.

"From the realm of eternal unity we chose frequencies, hues, and rates of vibration. Like crystals of snow forming in a stratospheric cloud, we personified them in the field of our common being. Our locations created space, our movements, time".[32]

We can say therefore that, as far as we can fathom, creation takes place along identical lines and that no one form of creation is so very different from another. Everything that exists is initially vibration with a frequency that is faster than the speed of light. The elements of the human body are the same as those that constitute this planet, and so we contain the history of its creation in our very chemistry. The basic pattern of the creation of the planet is the same as that of human beings. Our own gestation, in principle, is similar to that of the earth and of the cosmos. The source of our mental, physical, emotional and behavioural characteristics is to be found in the patterns which date from the beginning of time. Our gestation begins when this planet was a mere vibration, slowing down its frequency, and it ends when we utter our first cry. We are therefore intricately linked with all the movements of energy, in and out of time, space and matter, that are the dance of creation. Furthermore, we are the choreographer, the corps de ballet and the dance itself.

In the quiet garden the sun shone between the leaves of the tree forming a basket of light and warmth at its base, and inviting me to rest there. I sat down and placed my foot in my lap, imagining to myself that it represented the earth, with its gestation period reflected along the bony ridge on the inside of my foot. I had the idea that the power of life, which is manifesting as the earth, could resolve some of the problems created by mankind's crazy husbandry, and my intention was to act as a catalyst for that process. Within a few minutes, images of weird and wondrous travails assaulted my brain in such a way that I felt it wise to stop. It was as if I was witnessing the history of the earth's formation, which involved currents of energy of such power that there was a danger of short-circuiting areas of my brain, as if the synapses could not cope. I understood that the way I had thought of expressing my love and appreciation of the earth required a level of consciousness, of vibrations with a quicker and finer frequency, than the one that my emotional eagerness was able to manifest. As a novice swimmer I was attempting to swim the ocean!

The principle of vibration allows us to enter into the realm of pure movement, that is not the movement **of** something but movement *per se,* bearing in mind that nothing in the universe is at rest, and that everything moves and vibrates. This principle reveals how the difference between the myriad manifestations of matter, energy and mind results from the varying rates of vibration. In other words, "the universe is an infinite harmony of vibrating beings in an elaborate range of expansion-contraction ratios, frequency modulations, and so forth."[33] Everything in the world, therefore, receives its identity from the regularity of its movement of contraction and expansion.

"The materialising influence is the force of specified definition. It plays a central role in the creation and sustenance of the dimensional universe. Like frost drawing individualised ice crystals from the air, this influence draws crystallisations of basic molecular structure from the omnipresent energy currents of eternal love.

The materialising influence is the principle of contraction that holds energy efficiently bound in matter. It guides the eternal dynamics of matter and energy distribution in stars as well as the thermal and geological processes of planets like the earth. It is the quintessential materialising principle at its most basic level."[34]

"Love is the energy of expansion, the vital current of creation. When it touches matter lightly, the matter responds with life forms such as you have on the earth today. When it touches matter fully, stars are born."[35]

Expansion and contraction are two actions with varying degrees of expression between them. We may consider an object as being more or less cold or warm, according to our perception. Atoms, molecules, planets, suns and galaxies are in constant movement around each other, manifesting different frequencies and performing different functions. From one standpoint, something may appear to be as dense but from another standpoint it may appear to be extremely subtle. For example, different degrees in consciousness are to be found in nature's different kingdoms. If we look at the manifestations of life from the level of the vegetable kingdom, the animal kingdom will appear to be more evolved and subtle and the mineral kingdom will appear to be dense. From the standpoint of the human kingdom, on the other hand, the vegetable kingdom will appear to be dense. In the process of evolution, these different kingdoms have developed to express different levels of awareness, fulfilling specific functions. The vegetable kingdom, for example, can process the mineral kingdom, which we cannot do, transforming inorganic matter into organic matter. Try eating a bowl full of earth for supper as a means of feeding yourself with the minerals that your body needs! When we eat vegetables, we are truly partaking of the elements: earth, fire, water and air.

"The basic function of each being is expanding and contracting. Expanded beings are permeative; contracted beings are dense and impermeative. Therefore each of us, alone or in combination, may appear as space, energy or mass, depending on the ratio of expansion to contraction chosen and what kind of vibrations each of us expresses by alternating expansion and contraction. Each being controls his own vibrations." [36]

Given that there is consciousness at every level of manifestation, then every entity – every galaxy, every sun, every human being – controls its own vibrations. Expanded beings are permeative, that is to say they have the ability to penetrate other dimensions, while contracted beings are dense and impermeative, unable to do so. The former can act like steam, while the latter are more like ice.

When people start expanding from a contracted state of ill-being, difficulties and depression, they need some form of power. The highest power there is, their life force, is already at work. If they recognise that and allow their innate intelligence to take over, then transformation of the patterns begins to happen. However at this point the mind becomes frightened and will tend to try and make people return to the level of vibration on which they feel stable. Their life force and intelligence may shift that level of stability, – the level where they feel themselves to be comfortably at the same vibration with others, the level of the *status quo*, – towards a level that is more life encompassing. However that can only be done through an unresisting state of mind, through a constantly expanding love.

"No matter what your spiritual condition is, no matter where you find yourself in the universe, your choice is always the same: to expand your awareness or contract it. And you have to start where you are. There is nothing wrong with being where you are – it's one of the infinite experiences available to us."[37]

The movement of bending your arm is made up of two types of action: the contraction of certain tendons, ligaments and muscles and the expansion of others. The ratio of expansion to contraction will determine whether it is a quick or a slow movement. The slow movement can be compared to the creation of a human being, the quick movement to the formation of a supernova. The dual action of contraction and expansion when you bend your arm has, however, only one outcome; there is only one result, your arm bends.

Vibration stems from what we could call a pulse, – the pulse of life. And the differing ratios of contraction to expansion will allow new manifestations to come into being. In vibration, nothing exists as yet, but all possibilities are poised at the edge of the precipice of manifestation. There is as yet no time, no space, no matter or form, but the pulse is pregnant with the frequency modulations that will indeed give rise to matter and mind, forms and space with a duration in time. Vibration is movement, and movement without manifestation is a state of contraction and expansion at the service of creation. The movement of one level is the stillness of another level. This subtle domain that as yet has no material boundaries contains nevertheless the tracings, the templates of forms before they arise, the designs, so to speak, of the boundaries to come. And the form that emerges may be a human being, or it may be a cosmos.

How then does it all happen? If we go back to our spinning top, let us visualise how, with it turning so fast, the friction against the air has made it hotter. We perceive only a swirl of colours. As the movement decreases, we begin to hear a tone that gradually decreases in pitch as the top comes to a rest: from light to colour to sound to manifestation all within the matrix of movement.

The gospel according to John opens with: "In the beginning was the Word,..." We could say: "In the beginning was the Big Bang". The vibration of each entity forms its own energy pattern: rocks, insects, plants, all differ from each other because of their vibrational rate. "Sanskrit is supposedly the oldest language which evolved through the sound emerging from the sense of a thing's innate energy or vibration. Thus language evolves with the consciousness resonating with the being of things and often their kinaesthetic quality e.g. "stop" has an abrupt quality and "start" has a sense of acceleration in the sound."[38]

"In the beginning was the Word" means that the universe came into being through the vibration in its very nature. The "Word" is indeed sound, vibration, and movement. The spoken word is a vehicle of power, giving form and expression to thought. By verbalising a thought, we set in motion the forces that will create specific circumstances. The magnetism inherent in a thought verbalised acts as the cloak of a bubble that allows precipitation of understanding helping the spoken word on its way to the physical world of matter, influence and activity, resembling for example the surface tension of a drop of water.

The spiritual interpretation of the introductory words of the biblical gospel of John (John 1, 1-5), "In the beginning was the Word" obscures the inner meaning: In the primordial essence is the Word or light or the great creative thought, which conveys a greater significance.[39] Not only do we find in it the roots of two universal principles: that of creative impulse and that of vibration but also an illustration of the essence of consciousness, which cannot be fixed anywhere in time, even at the beginning. The 'Word' is not only representative of the creative impulse but also of the actualisation of the idea through vibration, which is the setting in motion, in the dimension which is out of time, space and matter, of the eventual materialisation of all things. The creative impulse (see the next chapter), as it generates of itself a back and forth motion, becomes consciousness which is the principle of vibration at work, that is a "displacement from," or a "departure of," the absoluteness of its balanced condition. And the spiralling apparition of shining manifestations becomes tangible echoes in the orbits of the subatomic particles, all suffused with consciousness.

The so-called differences between the various manifestations of the universal power are due entirely to their varying rates and modes of vibration. What we call matter or energy are but modes of vibration. All particles of matter are in a constant circular movement, be it corpuscles or sounds. The molecules of which matter is composed are in a state of constant vibration and movement around and against each other, in the same way as atoms and electrons. Each molecule of the body is held in its place, keeping its relationship with all the other molecules, because of its programmed frequency.

During a weekend seminar which I was giving, the whole group came spontaneously into a silence in which we remained for quite a while. I was totally absent. Then someone asked a question and I found myself, without meaning to, answering in a very rough voice. The content of the answer was fine but the way in which the answer was given physically, through the voice, was very gruff and abrupt. I realised that my body aspect was not functioning at the same level of empathy and loving vibrations inherent in the answer. The group did not notice it but the disparity was such that it produced a weird feeling in me. I could hear myself speak but it was from the dimension out of time, space and matter in which I seemed to be at the moment. I understood then the importance of educating the body because so much of oneself is now called upon to exist and to function consciously in both dimensions, in as well as out of time, space and matter. There is a greater need to be in both "places" at the same time. There are two structures: linear and global. In the dimension which is out of time, space and matter, the matrix is immediately there, totally so. This global awareness is concomitant to a movement of focalisation of its inherent power, which will bring manifestations into being, in time, space and matter. This is why we need to refine our body consciousness so that we may inhabit both dimensions "at the same time."

* * * * * * * * * *

From Einstein we know that space is curved and that this curve becomes greater in the presence of objects which have a greater density. In other words, space varies according to the density of the object that serves as a framework for that space. The more the density, the greater the curve, till a loop is formed which encloses that space. The black hole is a manifestation of that loop in which all energy is absorbed. It is said to contain a record of everything that has ever happened since the beginning of the universe. Could it be that this memory was fully expressed in the moment of your conception, when two cells united and became, at your birth, twenty thousand billion cells? Every single atom and cell of our bodies, of your body has been directed by a programme which we call the genetic code, and which would appear to be nothing other than memory. The initial creative impulse, actualised through vibration, is within each one of these cells, molecules and atoms.

"Relax into the awareness that lives in the genetic structure of your cells, the awareness that has long been waiting for admission into your thoughts. Open to the design pattern in which you are conceived, the original vision of your incarnate perfection, the archetypal vibratory envelope of eternal awareness that has individualised *as you* in this locality. Accept it, welcome it, awaken to awareness of your home."[40]

Discoveries in New Physics show that we can no longer separate or differentiate between matter and energy, as the atoms, considered as waves, as zones of influence, would appear to be nothing other than whirlpools of energy. Molecules for example, oscillate at the rate of twelve thousand billion per second and different electrons make between two hundred thousand and six million billion revolutions around the nucleus of their different atoms. This gives an idea of the extraordinary intensity of movement that is going on in each cell of your body. This movement is the manifestation of the unique reality that is the basis of the universe - vibration.

Let us listen to who we are truly. Not carried along by the specific waves of the manifestations of the mental states to which we may happen to vibrate in the moment, let us find, in the perfect equilibrium of this initial, primordial silence, the roar of creation that became the whimper of the Big Bang, a sonic boom in reverse. After all, are we not that consciousness? To consciously hear the sound of consciousness, is this not part of the purpose for which we are on earth as human beings? For, each cell has its own signature key, each organ, each limb, as many musical phrases of the great symphony of a human being, the body of humanity participating at its level in the music of the spheres. The great composer Beethoven knew the music of the body. Doesn't Mozart resonate in the heart?

"You will remember that everything has a soul song that is at once its definition and its expression. You will recognise all that lives in this blessed biosphere – and much more besides – as objectifications of your own melodies, and consciously then you will sing the Songs of Distinction, the songs that call forth all that appears in this planetary environment.

A sculptor can always use hammer and chisel, but if she sings the right songs, the songs that speak the true names, the songs that go to the very heart of the matter with which she works, she can inspire that matter to participate intelligently in its own development and re-creation. The matter will do more than conform to her conceptions; it will surpass her conceptions with ideas and suggestions of which she had never dreamed."[41]

Just as in a musical instrument there is resonance between the strings, so our thoughts and our emotions resonate to the thoughts and emotions of the people who are vibrating at the same rate as us – those who are "on the same wave length". This produces such phenomena as telepathy and the wonderful inventions which can result from the flashes of intuition which are sometimes experienced simultaneously in different parts of the world.

We have to start from where we are, recognising all the qualities, the so-called positive and negative, that colour the very fibres of our being, and letting them be, without judging them or attempting to manipulate them. We can simply realise that at times we may feel extrovert, outgoing, expansive, whereas at other times we may want to withdraw from the outside world and be "at home" within ourselves. The willingness to change can be synchronised, then, with our higher human motives and transformation can occur. The principle of resonance applies to literally every kind of vibrational interaction. We should therefore express the highest human qualities - such as attention, detachment, courage, compassion, loving concern, wisdom and inner silence, which are the natural attributes of intelligence and consciousness - with regard to our characteristics. They will then begin to resonate with the fields of energy which are in harmony with our true nature, and start vibrating to a new way of being by freeing their potential.

We know that everything in the world takes its identity from the regularity of its movement of contraction and expansion. When something is named, then that something acquires a separate identity. Again a resonance is at work. Instead of naming a symptom, a problem or a movement of so-called positive or negative energy in ourselves, let us simply consider these things as manifestations of energy that can transform themselves from within. That energy can then express a dynamism that draws to the manifestation what is necessary to find its own way of release and transformation, from the level of consciousness at which it is vibrating to a finer one.

We can now understand the importance of detachment, because being aware of manifestations and letting them be allows them to move and develop transcendentally from the lesser to the higher. We see this development in nature, from the seed to the plant, from the zygote to the human being. During our own gestation, we acquire all the characteristics that constitute a human being, and this process is overseen by the consciousness that we are. Some of these characteristics may be awakened earlier or later in our lives, or indeed not at all. We are therefore totally responsible for who we are and this enables us to fully realise our potential as human beings. Beware the mind that tends to go for the lesser, for the least appropriate thing.

By studying the principles that regulate us, we can become increasingly aware of the importance of letting the energies find their own level of vibrations, their own direction of release and transformation that is contained within their very dynamism. If we do not attempt to give any meaning or direction to the energies of the facts, then we are left with the facts in all their nakedness and we realise that facts are nothing other than truths, our understanding of which being limited to the level of perception at which we are functioning. These facts can transform themselves from within just as the caterpillar turns into the butterfly, presenting to the consciousness facts that had previously been inaccessible to us. We realise also that today's truth may be tomorrow's error as the level of consciousness changes. Detachment can then be seen to be of paramount importance.

If what we perceive is nothing other than ourselves, that is to say our own vibrational energy, then when the level of perception changes, a new reality begins to operate. When there is a state of contraction, the cosmic energy cannot trigger the transformation of an internal event as readily as when there is a state of expansion. Contracting to the extreme creates enormous density, expanding to the extreme allows dispersion. But love can move beyond and include all that. Physicists say that there are millions of waves that we are not yet able to recognise, material waves that are not physical and that may pertain to other levels of reality. These waves and particles are constantly moving through us, be it electromagnetic waves or neutrinos. Neutrinos have no mass but their action is fundamental as they seem to operate on the ultimate structure of matter at the subatomic level. As more space is created, it is possible that the action of this energy may be more manifest. It is said that seven hundred billion neutrinos move through each square centimetre of the body per second.

How can we avoid being caught in the continuous process of 'accumulation', in the mental tendency to add to the mass of data that we are? In other words, is it possible to move from a state of "having" to a state of "being"? We seem to be involved, at an unconscious level, in the cultivation of continuous feedback. This, however, produces for us two types of tyranny: the tyranny of knowledge and the tyranny of experience.

A friend and I were walking along a promontory when suddenly we caught sight of the Mediterranean sea sparkling in the sunset. We were silent, lost in the beauty. Then my friend said: "It is very beautiful but it is not the Mediterranean that I know". The words were like a scythe, shattering for me the suspended moment. She was comparing all the elements of that moment - the Mediterranean sea, her joy at being there and seeing that beauty, with her past experience of it. The mind was taking over the energy of that moment, saying that it did not want her to be lost in it, that it wanted to keep control. The mind relentlessly pursues power and employs these two forms of tyranny to maintain the *status quo*, and to prevent the individual, its ultimate supply of power, from changing. No amount of knowledge or experience will speed up or trigger the transformation of the caterpillar into a butterfly. This movement, natural, automatic and unconscious from its very beginning, is the effect of the movement of the very life energy of the caterpillar realising its potential in and as the butterfly.

In the 1940's in the United States, Professor Harold Saxton Burr[42] experimented with images formed in the energy field around seeds, and discovered that the image obtained was of the plant that would eventually develop from the seed. What prevents us from 'fulfilling', in the silence of the heart, the "image" that we are, the image that overshadows us and from which we have materialised? It is the mind that is constantly preventing this from happening in its attempt to retain supremacy over the human being. This 'upstart' tool, which is derived from our ability to know that we know, obviously has its role in the evolution of the universe, but it seems to consider itself as an independent entity, rather than a mechanism to serve human beings.

In order to keep control, the mind employs three elements that are simply projections into the future derived from the knowledge that it has acquired from the past. These elements are fear, hope and the more insidious one, belief, which is a wilful cultivation of ignorance. The three of them are as constrictive as attachment to knowledge or experience. To hope, to believe, or to fear is to assert that one does not know. If belief or hope and fear are seen simply as tools for accumulation of knowledge, then it is possible to rest in the realisation of who one truly is and a movement of knowing comes into being, rendering these tools obsolete. Collecting facts impedes and even prevents the movements of energy from coming to their rightful home. The knowledge of the scientist has put man on the moon but it has not changed him.

You set out one sunny autumn morning to walk across the hills to the forest of deciduous trees. The russet carpet of leaves echoes the warm glow emanating from the trees. Your heart partakes of the beauty, peacefully joyous. You stop half way up the side of a hill, overwhelmed by the splendour surrounding you. You stand still, utterly silent. There comes a ripple of energy at the surface of the consciousness, clothed in the words: "There is one more tree in the forest." The state of suspension is total. The trees move in the wind. This rooted body sways. At one point there is the perception of the movement as well as of the setting sun. You are thrown to the ground, suddenly struck by the fear that the mind generates: for these few precious hours, it had not exercised control. You understand this as you hurry home before the darkness is complete, carrying in you the knowledge of the joy and the glory of the day.

It appears that for the universe to go on expanding, there has to be biofeedback as well. The history of the universe could be defined by the word 'accruing'. If, however, there is no attachment to either state, contraction or expansion, then the vibrations become finer and the perception of different worlds or realities follows, till there is a realisation that all these perceptions are nothing other than oneself. In the words of J.

Krishnamurti: "The observer is the observed". Could there be a moment when your consciousness realises that it is neither this nor that, that all the different spheres of existence are nothing but waves on the surface of life?

I had been overworking, driven by ambition and mental projections, and a tremendous pain had developed in my back. That particular day, there was some kind of absent-mindedness in me and there arose in me attention to the pain. The pain was the fact, a manifestation of energy. There was only perception of the pain. It was so, a fact, without any movement in the mind to do anything about it, to get rid of it or to flow with it. The pain was the fact. There was attention to the pain. The pain was then felt more strongly, a naked type of pain.[43] There was attention to that. Deeper and deeper layers of the pain came up to the level of my perception, as if an onion was being peeled. Attention went on but without any mental movement. Layers of pain fell to reveal finer layers till there were none left. From the very core of the pain, there came a burst of light, at the very centre of that aggregation, which it dissolved. The convergence of forces that was the pain in the back revealed its true nature: light. There was a quiver in every cell of my body, an exquisite, instantaneous wave. The energy of attention had met with the energy at the core of the pain, and with it came the uncovering of the true nature of energy which at our level is light.

Suddenly the whole body was infused with that light. And so it is that attention is action. The relationship between power and consciousness is transformation, which is transmutation into a finer substance. I saw that transformation has an in-built mechanism that is communication. It was not just the pain itself that was transformed but everything to do with the pain, and this brought about insights into the nature of striving and mental power that had created the pain in the first place. There was no ego involved, no feeling of "I" taking over, no mind. Only the pain, and the attention. And the light.

As the energies of the facts transform them from within, these transformations lead us to perceptions of patterns beyond patterns in our everyday life and to a conscious alignment with these patterns. Every realisation is imbued with a dynamism that must be, and indeed is, translated into reality and into actual change in the modes of our behaviour. It is thus that our actions become impeccable.

* * * * * * * * * *

The principle of vibration reveals the source of movement expressed at three specific levels. The first level is concerned with the displacement of an object in time and space, be it the movement of a galaxy or the bending of an arm. As we have already discussed, if I bend my arm, the very action is the result of a movement of expansion and contraction of different muscles with more or less speed. The ratio of contraction to expansion of the muscles will create the action.

The second type of movement is a movement of transformation in nature. We can see it at work in the seed transforming itself into a plant, in the caterpillar turning into a butterfly, and in the joining of sperm and the ovum to create a conscious human being. That movement is inscribed, as it were, in the starting point of a being or an event and finds its self-fulfilment in its realisation. It is what human beings have yearned for since the beginning of time and it is at the basis of all the great religions. It is a yearning and a nostalgia for our true nature. However, as the Buddhists have intimated, it is still subject to the mechanical and the linear, as this transformation happens automatically, without conscious effort and naturally. Transformation is nothing other than the dying of forms so that other forms may come into being. In contraction as well as in expansion, there has to be a letting go of the patterns that these activities manifest. At the basic level, when one is cold, one tends to contract one's body. At a subtler level, when one is angry, there is also contraction, as opposed to the expansion which is found in the person who is in a state of love. We must learn, however, to allow the death in us of both dense and expanded states in order for the third type of movement to take place.

With this third type of movement, we are no longer concerned with form, or with the formless, but with the movement of life itself, as a constantly renewed creative impulse, out of time, without cause, unconditioned. It has no support or specific direction in time and space, transcending these domains, containing them and dominating them. This movement IS and is sufficient to itself. The two other types of movement are included in this movement.[44] It is said to be the realisation that one is the Source. Welcome home, lighthearted one.

Summary

The principle of vibration is a bridge between the transcendent dimension - one may call it God or Cosmic Creativity - and the universe.

It appears that a timeless, infinite energy, unbound by space or conditions, somehow "wishes" to create. There must be a bridge or connection between this "wish" and the material from which and in which living creatures are born.

The creating thought behind the cosmos focuses and gives birth to an apparently infinite range of hues, frequencies, and vibrational patterns. These patterns become more concrete in the myriad subtle and gross forms with which we are familiar: not only planets, trees, and animals for example, but also ideas, aspirations, and levels of consciousness.

Each individual, every relationship, every cell has its own unique vibration, characterised by the ratio of contraction and expansion.

The deepest transformation entails movement to finer and finer vibrations - closer to the frequency of pure light and liberation. This movement is achieved by an inner release of energy that was, perhaps, previously blocked and contracted.

The release is partly psychological but may be experienced at a more profound level with a change in the vibrational rate at the biological level, within the cells of the organism.

CHAPTER SEVEN

Know the thought you are and you know what you are beyond who you are

When we are considering reality and the different manifestations of matter, there are movements in our being that will lead us to search for and at times to recognise the patterns behind the obvious patterns that exist in time, space and matter. Outward appearances rarely satisfy us nowadays and there is an impulse within that makes us want to lift ourselves out of this mass of data that seems to constitute our everyday reality. We will look for the essence of things, questioning the nature of reality itself and seeking what lies behind it.

"The principle of mentalism", as I understood it from the Kybalion, was an expression used by Hermes Trismegistus more than 3000 years ago. I prefer to call it the principle of the creative impulse, so that we avoid the tendency to connect it with mental and intellectual pursuits. These are the end product of a vast realm of thoughts and concepts, which float in abstract space before they are clarified, brought onto paper and given form. Furthermore the formulation of ideas into their succinct and final form is accompanied by the tendency to classify them as living "objects" with words that are really only symbols. Ideas are living things and therefore subject to change and transformation; even though we can study and recognise their patterns, they are not fixed. And the patterns they describe are for ever changing in the dance of creation that is the play of consciousness, of vibration.

Let us echo the poet who wrote: "That thou canst not stir a flower Without troubling of a star".[45]

We realise now that we are actually and in reality one with the whole universe, that we are the microcosm, an infinitely minute reflection of the infinite universe, and truly the vast macrocosm. Given that eternal laws of harmony and beauty regulate the universe, if we align ourselves with the workings of its universal principles, so can we bring our lives into harmony and peace.

In the living of our lives, we call mostly upon the left hemisphere of the brain, the mind that is perpetually active and restless as a fretful child. We apply our minds to solving our personal problems but because it is limited, it will provide us with solutions which are apt to lead us into further problems and difficulties. When the mind is spontaneously still and we can take a broader perspective, we discover that the mind is indeed a very limited instrument, rooted in time, space and matter, in memory and storage of data, in association and in duality, and we see also that the problems we battle with concern not only ourselves but the whole of humanity. What is the nature of the reality that the mind perceives?

The word "reality" comes from the Latin "res", meaning "thing". By extension we can include in reality the material world as well as the subtle one of thought forms and emotions. In that context, the world of mind and its projections is real but transitory. What appears as a stable world, tangible, audible and visible, is but an illusion. New discoveries in Physics are showing us that matter is a dynamic, continuous movement of energy.

The line of demarcation between the world of our reality and the dimension from which it issues becomes blurred when we try and use the mind to delve into a world beyond itself, and ask it by means of words, reason and logic to grasp intimations of knowledge and insights to which it is totally alien. We can imagine the difficulties a foetus would have if it were asked to describe, explain and justify such concepts as the lungs and the respiratory system, given that it has no notion of air, knowing only the aquatic existence of the uterus. If the embryo realised that its energy would be called upon in the creation of such systems, it might even rebel. We are constantly reaching out and trying to peep round the other side of the Big Bang!

We have previously discussed in chapter six the three stages of purpose, idea and design which an object usually has to go through before it appears in time, space and matter. In the mind of the architect, in the realm of possibilities, the thought of the house did exist, whether or not the house was ever built. The purpose of the house was to provide somewhere for people to live. This eventually gave the dynamism to draw the plans and to bring about the building of it. There are factors affecting the actual construction, which belong in the realm of the abstract, and yet without them the house would never exist. Without the original thought, the building would never have existed.

Are we to think that human beings are mere expressions of a thought? That we are nothing more than tiny thought vortices in the intelligent flow of the river of life? And that a tiny amoeba or a vast cosmos comes into being in the same way? There is awareness at every level of manifestation, from the level of elementary consciousness of a frog to the more complex one of a human being. But we, human beings know that we know. To know the thought "I am" is to know "who I am" and beyond that, to know "what I am". We can recognise therefore the importance of the ancient Greek injunction: "Know thyself". How does this knowledge come into being?

The answer to this question may provide us with a key to the fulfilment of our purpose here on earth, which is to realise our potential as human beings. This tendency of being is constant, and creates a magnetic pull which means that there is a direction to our energies, towards realisation, fulfilment and enlightenment. This direction of energy is always in us. In the same way, in the acorn there is the necessity to create an oak, which the acorn inevitably does provided that it is alive and falls in the right environment.

Enlightenment is the goal that many people feel we should aspire to. To "enlighten" means to illuminate, to give light to or, figuratively, to impart knowledge, wisdom or spiritual light to someone. Let us then enlighten ourselves as to the nature of consciousness, of the creative impulse and its two feedback phenomena, and finally seek an answer to the question of whether there is a place in the body where the creative impulse will manifest.

His extraordinarily fine perception enabled Zarathustra to feel the energy field that coalesced into objects, and he called this the spirit. Towards the end of his life he would add that the spirit manifested to him in the form of light, saying: "When you drink of the stream, ask the spirit of the stream to partake of its water." He recognised the actuality of the principle of creative impulse.

In the Hebrew tradition God is seen as being omniscient, all knowing. From the current scientific perspective, this is recognised in the scientists' assertion that energy is consciousness. We are a compacted form of energy. The more compacted a form is, the more atomic energy there is in that form. Given that energy is consciousness, we are therefore a dense, compacted form of consciousness, which makes it difficult for us to access our truth and the truth of the cosmos directly.

Consciousness is vibration, which, as far as we are currently able to understand it, is light and sound. Through the principle of vibration, we know that a certain ratio of contraction to expansion will result in a specific manifestation. The dynamic instability within the movement of vibration caused the Big Bang which was a way in which life celebrated itself as the cosmos by taking a voice from the myriad possibilities within its blue print, passing from the unmanifest to the manifest.

And that celebration is happening now, in you, in me. Listen to the echo of the Big Bang every time you breathe? With each inhalation, there is the transformation of the subtle body of air and prana into your own body. Inhale, there is a strong accent; exhale, there is a weak accent. The song of our being, our own signature key, is not only an echo of that celebration but also a conscious rephrasing of the cosmic symphony. Where from comes the silvery shimmer on the spider's web in the dawn light? Using the bridge of your consciousness, it may have formulated itself out of your perception at dusk the previous evening of a play of light on the waves of the sea: your consciousness celebrating itself...

The mechanism which is inherent in the creative impulse is operating in two ways, the immanent and the transcendent. The immanent way starts from who we are, that is our body, mind, emotion, personality, and behaviour, the transcendent stems from the source of light that we are. But who are we?

There was a softness in the evening air as it came through the windows of the small Parisian apartment. The dinner party was very quiet and harmonious, each of us contributing to the conversation in terms of his or her own truth. The mother joined us from an adjacent bedroom, having put her baby down to sleep. The food was simple and delicious. The baby started crying. The mother went to him but the baby kept on crying his heart out. The father went in and the mother came back to the table, unable to explain the sobbing. I then finally went to relieve the father so that he could finish his meal. The baby was in my arms and his pain was immense. He was all pain, and cries. And I was there, just there, holding him in my arms. Suddenly there was this taste of nostalgia and beyond it a knowing. I talked inwardly to the baby:

"Yes, I know," I said. Opening his eyes, the baby looked at me startled, as if he had just woken up. I repeated in myself: "I know, yes, I know." He stopped crying. He kept on looking at me and with big sighs would start sobbing again but now not so desperately. I felt that he was crying out of the realisation that the whole of his being had just left a sublime dimension and had started suffering, obliged to live within the limitations of matter, yearning to go back whilst realising his inability to do so. Later, curled up in his mother's arms, he finally went into a deep sleep, sighing from time to time but undisturbed by the conversation around the dinner table where we had joined the others. When babies are crying, there may not always be a physical reason for it.

There is a pain that stems from the nostalgia for another dimension in which one constantly abides but which one tries to perceive from the point of view of time, space and matter. We hold on to the memory of something without realising that this something is actual, is now. It is therefore impossible to experience it truly from the standpoint of our everyday life with its limited perception except in those great moments where one is transported into some kind of ethereal "space" so to speak, those moments when the mind is absent.

The pain that is experienced stems from the separation that the mind creates between the fact, as we perceive it, of our being in time, space and matter and the realisation that essentially we belong to these domains out of time, space and matter, domains of which great beauty and objective love give us an intimation.

I repeat the question: who are we? Prisoners caught in the limitations of matter, time and space, suffocating in this cell whose iron bars block the vista on the other side of the window, happy within the context of the chains of repetitive action and reaction to polish the bars till they shine at the sunset of our life. And yet, we have this strange yearning. At times we catch a hint of the scents of other dimensions, which can cause us pain like that felt by the baby in Paris. Immediately we create a belief system that gives us the feeling that we are alive, and we accept being defined and affirmed by other people's systems, not listening to our own truth, involving ourselves in futile behaviour that is supposed to abolish the iron bars and produce nirvana!

Can we, without spiritual practices, without setting goals, bring ourselves to a point in "choiceless awareness" at which we can experience the nature of that energetic understanding? Beyond knowledge and mind, there is a state, within the silence of the heart, a state without attributes or qualities, that is the fount of all knowledge and understanding, the very source of the creative impulse. The caress of this state of knowing reveals to us that the iron bars, the walls of the prison, the very matter that weighs us down, are the elements that serve as fuel to propel us into these other dimensions that we are. Love them, love them!

I stayed on at the community meeting to make sure that there would be no further attempt to manipulate the young woman who had confided her feeling that she no longer wanted to participate in the group meetings.

There had already been a lot of manipulation along therapeutic models, with therapists stressing that she had a responsibility in terms of the group energy and questioning her action. She was distressed and before the community meeting had asked to talk to me about it. She had resolved her dilemma within herself, but did not know how to express it. She had understood the importance of saying no to being involved with her group and the whole community. I pointed out that instead, she could say yes to herself, a kind of existential yes that was very important as an expression of her own inner authority. In this case there was no need for manipulation, justification or explanation. The only important thing was to feel that it was right for her, that she was expressing her own truth. At the end of the community meeting, where the issue was brushed aside, people started gathering in their own smaller groups. She stayed on and called for attention: "There are three groups here and I am part of a fourth group that is the group that doesn't attend any group. And so good-bye!" Zero group. And she left. She remained part of the community but as a guest now instead of a member. Creative action with inspiration in the moment!

We are fulfilling our purpose here on earth in a unique fashion. Our role in the cosmos is first to express consciousness of consciousness by embracing, in consciousness, the two dimensions that we are, the one in and the other out of time, space and matter. Through the dynamic play of the void and plenitude, everything, including consciousness which is aware of itself vanishes. This dictates how the understanding of everything that exists in time and space may appear without limitation in our consciousness. Through the heart via intuition and inspiration, a restful presence fully at home in every dimension, we may ride the steed of the creative impulse if that is what in the moment is required. What is its nature?

Ideas are living entities, specific vibrations of energy. What is the process that allows a thought at large to become your thought that you can then express? "I have had an insight!", someone will exclaim. How is the subtle energy of a thought "captured", as it were? There are a few steps involved.

In order to come into manifestation, the very fine energy of a thought vibration is lowered into a light form. The electromagnetism of the energy field in and around your body attracts it according to the nature of your thought processes and emotional state of the moment. Through observation, I have realised that the place in the body in which the creative impulse anchors itself is the pineal gland. It receives this light that then goes into the pituitary gland, which assesses its frequency and transforms it so that, through the spinal fluid and the nervous system, it can imbue each and every cell of your body with its knowledge. The same process is repeated at the microscopic level, the cell being a reflection of the light body and the electromagnetic field surrounding the human body. We may assume that the same movement goes on at the atomic level and so on, *ad infinitum*. This is called the vertical movement.

To put it in a wider context, the cosmic intelligence expresses itself as universal knowledge. In order for that knowledge to incarnate as you or me, it needs to "die" to itself. The knowledge *per se* slows down its frequency to become a vibration. Meaning and order which are inherent in the working of the principle of creative impulse, are present when the unmanifest becomes manifest, that is in the movement from the timeless, spaceless and formless to the realm of time, space and matter. It follows from this that necessity and purpose give the moving energy its direction; they are the underlying factors that will "cause" the slowing down of the energy that is then released in the form of light.

The energy field in and around your body, the whole of you and your attributes, all exercise a strong magnetic attraction on all the elements which are necessary for the fulfilment of your purpose in a unique way. The light hits the pineal gland. There is inspiration. Suddenly you know. Not only you but the whole of you, your body, all the cells know. A deep understanding, one without words, pervades everything. There is knowing.

When Dr. Gustav Jung was asked whether he believed in God, he appeared not to want to answer the question. When the interviewer insisted, there was a pause, and then the answer came, with great humility: "I know." There was such dynamism, such tremendous power in that answer.

A wonderful and elaborate feedback operation comes into play as the lesser incarnated knowledge refers back to the greater original creative thought that has given it form and substance, the ray returning to the light of its origin. If everything emanates from thought, then everything sends the thought of its being back to the thought that is its origin. The creative impulse is self-sustaining and if this feedback continues, you go on being creative.

For the feedback to sustain itself, a person needs to be well grounded. If the principle of gender is well integrated, then the feedback has a kind of boomerang effect and the greater the integration with the masculine-feminine principle, the greater the boomerang effect will be. The incarnated energy will refer back to the energy *per se.* The vertical feedback that allows the entire body and its cells to feel the creative impulse is not just knowledge in the mind, but knowledge throughout the whole body. If that doorway remains open, the creative impulse goes on happening and the whole of your life becomes a creative act.

Artists and other creative people experience this spontaneously when they are linked to their creative power. Very often their ability to be attentive to their inner prompting, their perseverance, their endurance and their sensitivity will be matched by a certain groundedness that keeps on feeding them with the power they need to carry on being creative. Their paintings or their works of art may reflect who they are. At other times they may indeed be expressing a vision which accords with the energies around the earth or the energies of the moment, heralding for humanity an opening at the level of global consciousness.

Just as a creative and imaginative choreographer intuits new steps and variations for the dancers, using their living power to in-form his masterpiece, and allowing the audience to partake in the glory of soaring to heights of beauty and nobility, so the ultimate designer, which is what we are at the level of oneness with the source, thinks up the universe in all its beauty in harmony with the loving power with which it vibrates. Matter, energy and forces operate in accordance with that part of our nature which regulates these levels by means of laws. The fact that we can know the principles which are the basis of these laws indicates that there is a function in humans that is a reflection of that function in the universe which is performed by the ultimate designer. The principle that allows us as designers to know and to think up the universe is that of creative impulse.

An empty hole is swinging up in the air
And the fullness of its absence calls me up to it
I reach out to its other side
It is even emptier
Its echo whispers into my ear
Try the other side of my other side
Without rhyme or reason I dive into it
To find myself at the horizontal
Of the vertical where I was before
Before what
Before the time when an empty hole was swinging up in the air
Calling me up to it by its absence.

Anyone - the secretary, the artist, the person who

washes the dishes, - can express the creative impulse in everyday life. Whatever the activity, the quality of the attention and the quality of being will show through, laser like. The artist paints the picture and does not know how it is that he does it; it is just there. The creative process arises equally in the woman married to a composer, who shows her creativity through dealing with the housework and looking after their child. I like to sit and be with them. They were happy when they learned about the universal principles and started working with them, because it revealed the structure of their apparently structureless creativity, which at times had made them think that they were crazy doing certain things in the particular way they did. The way of creativity does not have a programme, or a recipe. They discovered that they had been working very much in harmony with the universal principles through their creativity.

In the state of knowing and creativity, the creator cannot make things happen or hold on to anything known or experienced. There comes this ability to carry on with the work in hand, because the creative source is constantly renewing the ability to create. We are told that Van Gogh was in the state that enabled him to paint a masterpiece such as "The Starry Night", for a long time. You need to be well grounded, however, to be able to contain such extraordinary power. "It is eating me up, this energy," he is quoted as saying. The key to that grounding lies in the principle of gender. (See chapter 1.)

Another type of feedback immediately arises in the mind of the cells of the brain at the moment when the creative impulse sheds its light, when knowing takes place, when a new and wonderful insight seizes our attention or enlightens our situation. The knowledge that imbues and penetrates all the cells of the body and the brain, awakens a resistance in the elementary consciousness of these cells, which might say, if it had a voice to express itself: " I don't know what is happening. I don't like it. This may be dangerous to my survival so let's stop it." This resistance will use an extraordinary amount of energy to put an end to the vertical feedback, so that the horizontal feedback can get under way. This causes the creative impulse to peter out, as if the circuit had been broken.

The horizontal movement of energy, the horizontal feedback, consists in the assessment of each new inner event, or thought, by the 'bank' of thoughts that is the memory. The dynamism inherent in that assessment produces mental associations which we call "thinking", a poor relation of the explosive, creative dynamism of the vertical movement. We prefer to think by association, instead of being creative and directly knowing because our instinct for survival demands that we proceed only from the known to the unknown. Fear is a projection of the mind. The fear of death – of a pattern, a habit, the human body or the ego for example – actively prevents creativity. Except when it is off its guard, the subjective consciousness filters and rejects the fine energy of the vibration of cosmic consciousness or creativity that threatens the *status quo*. Usually the mind with its appetite for control appropriates the energy of the creative impulse in that second feedback.

This horizontal feedback may be a blessing in disguise at times because it acts as a safeguard against the very fine yet powerful energies that our magnetism attracts. These energies may awaken atavistic memories that can overwhelm the psyche or simply short-circuit the electrical impulses in the brain if one is not adequately grounded.

The upheaval which the vertical feedback causes in the brain cells awakens a robotic mechanism that manifests through the horizontal feedback, because the creative impulse challenges the elementary consciousness of the cells. This mechanism will try to kill off that energy of creativity because it does not know, within its own parameters, the subtle level of the dance of life. The robot takes over and the creative impulse disappears.

We may well be ninety-five percent robotic. The robot is living our life for us. It is a very useful little device, this robot. It allows us to walk, for example. As children we learned how to walk and then very quickly the robot took over, the action becoming mechanical. We learn to drive and the robot quickly starts driving the car for us. When it comes to subtler things, however, the robot will continue to take over. You listen to a beautiful concerto that moves you to tears. You listen to it again; you are moved again. But then by the fifth time the robot will do your listening. It is the same thing with making love. You experience a wonderful wild night of love; you seek the same experience again, but fairly quickly the robot gets under the sheets. You become part of a couple and soon there are two robots who agree to be together and call it marriage. How are we to prevent the robot from having the upper hand? Stillness and attention are the means of counteracting this aberration. At times, the dimension out of time, space and matter that we are comes to the rescue and says in a small voice: "I am here. Don't forget that who you perceive you are is simply the tip of the iceberg. I am not only that tiny tip but also the ice below the water and more importantly all water everywhere. You are life, not just its manifestation!" As you become creative, you go less and less robotic.

A restful type of attention which we will discussed further allows the vertical feedback to go on happening. It brings about a constant realignment of the energy to that very strong current of the creative impulse. This resonance to the subtle movement of creativity cannot be achieved through meditation, which is itself a system. In creativity there is no structure because it is happening out of time, space and form. It is forever moving, like a gentle breeze. It is in the stillness of the spontaneously silent mind, which is not making any associations that the possibility arises for another dimension to express itself, that dimension from which come true knowledge and to a lesser extent, intuitive knowledge. And so in the silence, the energy is not directed in order to find knowledge. It propels you from the peaks of insight to the vast rolling plains of communication, from void to plenitude.

Knowing, the state of knowing belongs to a domain all of its own. It is connected with information arising spontaneously without any external trigger, streaming along pathways illuminated from the heart of knowingness. There is this feeling of something happening, of being informed, of life arising as yourself knowing the whole of life, as attention prevents the robot from taking over.

If you cut a skirt from a piece of cloth, the skirt will exist in time, space and matter but it still belongs to the world of the cloth. The cloth and the skirt are not different, the skirt is made of that cloth. We can compare the cloth to the out of time, space and matter aspect of everything and ourselves to the skirt, tailored in the energy of that aspect. In the same way, the ocean rises as the wave.

The mind creates the "I" that expresses itself as the ego that creates the belief that control is necessary in order for it to sustain itself. It wants to separate skirt from cloth, wave from ocean, you from life, by creating the tyranny of knowledge which can bring about the entropy of inertia. Because we think we know something, we do not pay attention any longer. The accumulation of information creates a kind of inertia that kills creativity.

"While it is appropriate for materialistic values to dominate atomic and subatomic realms, they become extremely destructive when they dominate human determination."[46]

Through knowing we can break free of the shackles of the mind and the inertia. Knowledge and knowing are two totally different things: knowing is the dynamic aspect, the creative action that brings forth knowledge:

"Ah, I know!" The principle underlying this movement is the principle of creative impulse.

The purpose of nature is fruitfulness. We are part of nature and produce our fruits, sperm and ovum. This is a cyclical phenomenon as this movement of change operates in time, space and matter. However, when we come to the movement of creativity, as human beings we can transcend this cyclical movement. Because we know that we know or that we can know we are able to free ourselves from the laws operating in time, space and matter, and consciously live for the love and the fulfilment of the Self which is our potential. If we consider the creative knowledge at the level at which it is given, without restricting it to the context of what we already know, so the ability to appreciate the potential is raised.

Because the mind uses the energy to sustain itself in the domain of matter, time and space, it will harness the energy locked in the vestigial instinct of survival in order to maintain the survival of the ego. The mind pursues this end to such a degree that it has devised the means to blow up the whole planet and itself in the process. Its absolute control ends with its own destruction. Do we need such survival instinct? We are at a stage in our evolution where the brain, a kind of cosmic foetus, is being asked to participate in the creation of elements that will operate in a dimension other than the one it has become accustomed to over the last few million years. These elements, these "organs" relate to the formless, timeless and spaceless dimension, and their creation is urged on, by the ever strongly felt energies which are manifesting according to the principle of creative impulse.

"What is the knocking?
What is the knocking at the door in the night?
It is somebody wants to do us harm.
No, no, it is the three strange angels.
Admit them, admit them."

D. H. Lawrence.[47]

The knocking at the door is the second method that the creative intelligence uses to manifest its transcendent eccentricity, and unable to contain itself any longer it is moving exuberantly into a new state, carrying us along into a new magnitude. As the possible receptor that we are reaches out in whatever way it can towards the cosmic celebration of creativity, the cosmic body communicates wondrous information, from the universal blue print creating even more means of celebrating itself. It interacts with our subjective consciousness and with our mind, whose movement is connected with the brain which will compare and judge information using the accumulated knowledge and experience of the past. It bypasses the heart and the heat waves of the sun to alight us at the fire of a new understanding, the light behind the light.

That light is love and so we are now able to look through its beams at the slowly dissolving images of self. We realised the importance of cutting the emotional ties that linked parents and children when we discussed the principle of gender. Now the dissolution is even greater as, in the glare of the loving light, the ties that bind us in illusion to the manifest world are released like a firework on the exploding, ever changing horizon of the knowledge of Self.

* * * * * * * * * *

We know, and that knowledge goes beyond any data from time, space and matter. We can know either by means of the senses or by means of the mind, performing activities in their possible or active perceiving or apprehending, either through understanding or comprehending. These abilities have their source in the state of knowing that belongs to the realm of light and light release.

To know does not necessarily mean that something can be put into words. However there is thought underlying all manifestations and if we can perceive or understand a thought without any verbal content, we are getting close to an understanding of the principle of creative impulse. To know directly with the senses is far better than knowing with the mind, because the light coming from the depth of a thought that "wishes" to become known in harmony with the needs of our being, irradiates the cells of the body. To have access to that sort of power means that our potential to be aware and to create is unlimited.

Francis Bacon understood this when he wrote: "Knowledge itself is power." John Keats went further: "Knowledge enormous makes a God of me." Dr. Serena Roney-Dougal writes: "Recently, neurochemists have discovered that the pineal gland makes a neuromodulator which is virtually indistinguishable from an alkaloid used by South American shamans and tribes for astral travelling, healing, divination, etc."[48]

Could the pineal gland be the bridge between spirit and matter, a biological receptor that translates higher-frequency information into language that the nervous system can recognise? Could enlightenment reflect an actual movement of energy in and around the pineal gland? It is known that this gland is sensitive to light, especially with regard to its production of the hormone melatonin which "... normally follows the light-dark cycle, with high levels at night and low or undetectable levels in the day. When mammals are maintained in constant darkness, the pineal rhythm of melatonin production runs free, with a periodicity of around 24 hours; that is, it becomes a circadian rhythm..."[49]

What is sleep? It is a function that allows the body to recover at a certain level. The actual physical recovery requires very little sleep. However the mind uses up so much energy at the expense of the body's requirements that we need much more sleep than we would if the mind was spontaneously still. Even mind-stilling practices use up energy. The actual physical movements that take place in the brain during sleep allow everything that has not been integrated during the day to be processed. This processing goes on in a weird manner but connections at an unconscious level are made between different events in our lives and at times we have insight into that in dreams. However, connections happen not only between things that we have experienced up until now but also with what is called the universal unconscious or the collective memory. The brain will use up a lot of energy in order to create an order with which it is satisfied but that order is not necessarily the truth. If your days are very still and your mind is almost absent whilst there is attention, without discrimination, to everything that arises, then you need very little sleep.

Continuous awareness is possible twenty-four hours a day if everything that happens during the day - not just what comes up to the level of the subjective consciousness - is processed, just observed and allowed to be. In this way the brain does not have so much to process at night. The body can be observed going to sleep and movements of dreams can be observed when they arise, but there is consciousness throughout. The dream is observed as a dream, then it stops and there is a state of absence again. After an hour or so the body itself is rested, so one can get up and start the day. Experiencing this made me understand that the requirements of the mind and the brain greatly condition the requirements of the body. The importance of this continued awareness needs to be emphasised, as it is one of the factors that enable us to take full responsibility for the body of light that we are.

In the past ascetics and mystics would seek to escape from the level of matter and form. We are now at a point in the history of our evolution as conscious beings where we need to embrace fully the matter of ourselves and everything around us. To affirm that we know that we know is to assert our responsibility: by embracing matter, we raise it to the level where it belongs, the level which it expresses in its yearning to awake. As if the chair on which you are sitting had insight into the idea of the designer and into the design that generated it...

To repeat Lorber's definition of John Sorpel's introductory words; "In the primordial essence, in the primal cause of all life was light, the great creative thought, the existential idea." As already mentioned in the previous chapter, some physicists are now in agreement with the mystics of the past and assert that matter is crystallised or frozen light. The principle of creative impulse recognises that all manifestations of life are essentially that light and that they issue from the primordial essence. The primal cause as creative impulse is a constantly renewed shower of sparkling beauty.

From the movement of intelligence that is the creative impulse issues consciousness, which is concerned with the manifest as well as the unmanifest. At a lower level, there appears another element which we call mind. We have the faculty of being aware with the attendant aptitudes for reflection, deduction, inference and reason. To a certain extent, the animal, vegetable and mineral kingdoms, and indeed the whole world of matter partake of these aptitudes. It is obvious that when consciousness is not hampered by mind it evolves its own action or movement in whatever situation.

We are this consciousness that has this further ability to be aware of itself, an energy moving through time and space without interruption, without boundaries. As the understanding of the possibility of that movement dawns on us, we realise that we have no power, no control other than that of the ultimate designer, designing the next piece of creation. We have the ability to feed ourselves with all the power and the love that we feel we need at this earthly level because we understand that we are free and continuous beings moving through its creation of time and space for the sheer joy of the experience. It is thus that our relationship with ourselves, the rest of humanity, with matter, with the cosmos and with all that is becomes ever more conscious as we rejoice in the manifestations of the creative impulse.

SUMMARY

Our daily world – the "real world" – appears physical, material, sequential. One event causes the next; objects impinge on other objects. At its most subtle, this world can be felt as vibration, the interplay of patterns of vibrations.

With creative impulse, we enter a new domain, the source dimension from which the daily world issues. In this new, ever-new domain, the parameters of space, time, matter, and causation do not apply. Instead, the domain is characterised by light, bliss, intelligence.

We live in the daily world, but we may remember, or intuit, the realm of light. Thus we feel a nostalgia and a yearning. Our deepest nature obliges us to move towards the light as a plant seeks the sun.

To approach an understanding of this Source, we envision it as having qualities: it is the Ultimate Designer, and it moves by Creative Impulse.

The creative impulse arises in the mind of the cosmic designer. Light somehow lowers its frequency, still retaining its integrity, to be immersed in our slower, denser realm. Matter and energy - crystallised light - perform the drama composed by the Creator.

This process can never be described adequately in words. For want of a better term we call it the principle of creative impulse.

How do we gain knowledge of the Source? If we set out on the path, our inner being exerts a "magnetic pull" to attract all the elements which are necessary for the fulfilment of its yearning. If we are creative and grounded, we start to express the cosmic mind; the cosmic mind would also appear to rejoice in this play.

These states may arise after periods of open-minded attention and receptivity. We also have the capacity to obstruct and foil our creativity. Robotic behaviour, endless conceptualising, greed, and confusion will apparently trap us so that we miss the glory.

Are we separate in essence from the Ultimate Designer, from the energies of light? I propose that the light behind our consciousness and the light behind the cosmos is one light.

Then we see that the manifested world also is never-bound. All is ever-free, ever-perfect. We embrace the manifestations and they disappear. The next moment of creation appears.

CHAPTER EIGHT

THE PRINCIPLE OF INSIGHT/ ILLUMINATION

May currents of insight illuminate your heart in the revelation of the one light

"One of the happiest moments of life comes in the split second where the everyday suddenly becomes the dazzling aura of the intensely new... These illuminations are too rare, more singular than regular; and we are caught most of the time in the everyday humdrum and the trivial. Even more horrible: what seems to be the quotidian is the matter itself of which the discovery is made. The only difference comes from our perspective, from our will to gather the pieces together in an entirely new way and to see a drawing in the very place where shadows stood a moment earlier." From Thinking in future Tense *by Edward B. Lindaman.*

"Do not suppose that I have come to bring peace to the Earth: It is not peace that I have come to bring but a sword."[50] With these words, Jesus affirmed the nature of his being: the Christ energy. The function of the sword to which he referred was to differentiate the vibrational fields that had overlapped and to stop the confusion between universal essential values and the materialistic ones which not only prevailed then, but are still with us today. There are two specific domains. There is the one that we know well that is in time, space and matter and in which principles are operating that regulate and maintain the physical universe as we experience it with specific laws, and then there is the domain of the cosmic light behind the solar light.

The bonding of all the different energies is essential, but

if the materialising influences prevail, their movement will bring about aberrant behaviour, with limiting and contracting characteristics, with everything becoming dense and impermeative, and, for human beings, diseases, problems, ageing and death will predominate. We have allowed laws operating in time, space and matter to exercise such a hold on our consciousness that the ego has become over-inflated, with the attendant states of fear, projection, defensiveness and the survival instinct becoming exaggerated. Can we shake off the domination of these materialising influences? Can we tear off the shackles of memory, experience and knowledge that is simply stored information?

It seems that matter, time and space have evolved under the sway of repetition and the acquisition of habits. Was something that at first proved useful and fruitful, destined to become dominant and stultifying? The mind will use the tyranny of experience and memory to keep control, creating an entropy through repetition. As we realise the importance of changing, we will adopt programmes of exercise or practices that are however formulated by the very mind that will sabotage the attempt with its investment in control. How to get out of that vicious circle? Light, through the principle of insight/illumination, will dissolve the patterns. The action of that dissolution is at the heart of the state of bliss.

Considering that the very cells of the body are alive, it would seem that the level at which they agree to manifest becomes a self-sustaining circuit of destruction which is ultimately self-defeating. The misguided willingness of the cells to maintain a specific level is due to their instinct for survival, which is nothing more than a projection of their own mental fear at an elementary level, and it is this which prevents the cells from realising their very potential, and from revealing their true nature of light, love and oneness. This survival instinct negates the generative void whose presence is the condition for the establishment of a finer order of consciousness and organisation, for the transformation into a new plenitude.

It was the first time that the children had been allowed to sleep in the great outdoors. The night was warm and the sky was sparkling with stars. One boy took his sleeping bag and withdrew from the giggling crowd. He lay with his back propped up against a dead tree trunk. He felt secure. He dared to peep out at the dark immensity and to sustain the blinking call of the stars. One of his hands gripped a branch, and the fingers of the other one clawed the earth in order to find an anchor. There was the danger of falling, of being sucked up. He held on with all the courage he could muster. Gravity went. A door opened. He was at the threshold. There was a chasm, a light shining, beckoning. "Are you all right?" a familiar voice asked. He fell into the welcoming arms, relieved that there were still humans around.

To understand the laws which operate in time, space and matter is to understand the infrastructure that keeps everything together; it is also to understand the illusion, which the Hindus call "maya". The evolutionary habit that is expressing itself through these laws seems to be acting like a net that becomes ever more constrictive as evolution, expansion and therefore proliferation continue. All attempts to escape will be made from within the net and will never be strong enough to break through the mesh. Fear, hope, systems of belief and of spirituality are the tools devised by the human mind to ensure the suicide of the race and the destruction of the Earth which human mismanagement is currently bringing about. Is it possible to get out of this state of affairs? Where can we find the energy to do it? Is there another perspective from which consciousness operates in a different way? Are we sleeping? Are we missing something?

"People don't see the power of thought, they think it is just some little thing ... but it has a tremendous emotional charge and a tremendous neurophysiological, neurochemical effect ..."[51] In order for there to be true conceptual education, there has to be a realignment of the energies of the emotional and physical levels. If we use the conceptual tools consciously and with precision, in the way that a cabinet maker uses his plane to allow the grain of the wood to emerge, then the new vibrational patterns that are currently active on the planet, and which are the principle of insight/illumination at work, can be truly manifest. This all started two thousand five hundred years ago with the actualisation of the Buddha energy field and it has gained momentum ever since.

Let us look at another domain. By attending to who we are truly, we realise that there are other principles operating but that these are out of time, space and matter. The energies and the dynamism of the events deriving from them are such that they can lift us out of this mass of data that is what we are at the material level. From the sun's perspective, everything is light, and there can be no shadow. If we realise that we are light, and every one of our cells is a being of light, then the laws operating in time, space and matter and duality lose their supremacy. And what happens in the sun will of course affect everything that its rays touch. This means that there is immediate action and transformation.

From the standpoint of the realm which is out of time, space and matter, from the standpoint of unity, there is absolute clarity of perception. This is the solution to our subjective thinking and consciousness and a morality is established which is not based on religious or social premises, a morality that engenders behaviour which is inspired by necessity or natural integrity. Life's necessity or purpose, we realise, is to fulfil the highest potential of all its manifestations. By understanding the principles operating out of time, space and matter, by being attentive to them, by acting accordingly, we break free of the net, of the proliferation and of our strangulation by matter and gravity.

A new world is in the process of being born, because the dynamism of the new laws awakening in the atoms, and the cells of our bodies pervades, activates and regulates the matter that we are. If we listen to the cells, get to know the laws and embrace their dynamism, if we agree to die to the biological, mental, psychological and physical forms that we are, if we agree to die to the habits and conditioning enshrined in our very cells, and if we die to past experience, memory and knowledge, then we can be renewed, we can be reborn. The butterfly does not cling to the memory, the conditioning, the consciousness nor even the bliss of being a caterpillar!

The teenager went to his bedroom in the boarding house where he lived. There was an unease in him that needed attention. Lying on his bed, he asked questions: Is it this? Is it that? The answers came, like gun fire. There was such a certainty. No, not that. This is finished. That is over. It was as if a laser beam were at work, scattering, dissolving, blowing to pieces all the assumptions, yearnings, dreams and desires that he saw for what they were. Even the oasis of a close relationship went, being found lacking. In what? The emptiness of being could find in it no consolation, no reassurance, no confirmation. There was nothing left. But then, where to? What? It was total void. There was complete emptiness, nothing to live for, though there was no despair, no depression. A perception finer than a razor's edge demanded total honesty; a penetrating, uncompromising assessment of all the aspects of his being was taking place, without judgement, commentaries or attempts at mitigation. It was total void. Nothing left. He lay on his bed, more naked than naked. The insights belonged to the domain of the absolute. A wave rising from the deep core of his adolescent self caught his attention. In puzzlement, he asked: Is that so? There was illumination in his understanding. The only thing left, he realised, was sex. The time had not come yet to stop the seeding. As the sacred act took place, he recognised the value of that anchor, the only one remaining to him at that moment.

As the universe expands physically, new principles move from the potential to the actual. Gautama, Jesus and Mohammed were all heralds of the awakening and the actualisation, in the realm of time, space and matter, of energies from another dimension, the essence of which is light, love and unity. The Buddha energy ushered in the principle of insight/illumination/revelation. It brought about the understanding and the overcoming of the laws of nature which pertain to mind, emotion and matter, loosening some of their materializing hold on spirit.

The man sat under a tree; he had been both a libertine and an ascetic. Nothing had satisfied his quest for understanding. There was no longer anything to do. As his energies were not now used to any particular end, they were at the disposal of his attention, which became keener. He perceived subtler forms of manifestations as the swing of the pendulum of polarity became shorter and shorter. Other spheres of existence revealed themselves to him, other dimensions that do exist but are still manifestations only at subtler levels of existence. "No, it is not this, no it is not that." Until the swing stopped. There was no pole anymore. He was totally immersed in the one energy that revealed itself, that revealed its true nature. Gautama became the Buddha. Through his enlightenment, he opened the way for every human being to realise their potential of light. He brought about the movement of the principle of insight/illumination/revelation from the potential to the actual. He established in the consciousness of mankind our right to access the information that is circulating in the unified field of vibrations, the right to access the consciousness that precedes all individualisation, the ability to tap into not only a body's complete genetic code that is contained in each of its cells but also into the secret light within each of the body's trillions of cells.

Then, there was actualisation. With the Buddha energy acting as a catalyst the blueprint of light was unveiled. Now seems to be the time for revelation, for the realisation that we are that light and that love in oneness, three forms of the same essence, manifesting at the core of matter which surfaces from fire, water and earth in the breath of life, indeed from the very cells of the human body. Our true nature is enshrined there and we are now awakening from the sleep of our present condition to the fulfilment of our destiny.

We have already considered the principle of vibration, that we can compare to the drawing of a designer, and the principle of creative impulse, which we compared to the thought of the designer or the creator. Already, this last principle involved aspects of light. In order for something to be created there has to be a purpose for it, which I define as "a movement towards something at the service of necessity". The language of light is the formulation of its purpose, which is to create, and create again, rejoicing in the multi-faceted expression of its necessity. The principle of insight/illumination/revelation, which we are now looking at, can be described as the fine crystallising power of creation poised on the edge of the manifestation of itself as thought or matter, on the point of releasing its energy in the form of light, shining with all its jewels of light as potential worlds, in accordance with its highest bliss.

The universal language of light does not have the same grammar as the language of possession that holds us prisoners to its structures. The living organic information that is imparted is a song with a harmony so sublime that it echoes in the heart of every living thing, specific, inclusive, concise, comprehensive and simple. Its overtones can be infinitesimal, its undertones vast, linking up and embracing in the arms of infinity. There are musical instruments and other means that can convey a hint of this sublime song. There is an instrument called the Monochord table on which you can lie while someone plays the 50 or so strings which are all tuned to two specific notes. This produces overtones and undertones that resonate with your body, healing you through harmonics.

How did we lose this living language of light? How did we come spiralling down the corridors of time and space? It would appear that as the universe continued to expand, more and more mechanisms with an ever increasing complexity were created. Energy and consciousness began to manifest as organisms which adapted and became ingenious materialising influences and thus duality took greater hold. This led to friction, conflict and, in the human being, to notions of past "guilt" and future "fear" with the energy of consciousness becoming increasingly dominated by the gravitational forces.

In the savannah of ancient times, people would rub two sticks together to produce fire and, with it, light. The energy created by friction, which arises from strife and conflict, however, is short-lived, because the clash of two opposing forces will eventually result in the annihilation of both of them. As we compare, imitate, identify with, and conform, we fuel conflict with our own living energies. By identifying with the past, for example, we get the feeling that we have accomplished something, so we can sustain a "good" self-image, and in this way we distort our perception of ourselves, losing touch with our own spirit and becoming unfamiliar with the reality of our nature. In other words we are living a myth and not our own life.

Are we lured by the peace of the mineral kingdom, that is, after all, part of our own basic structure, to cultivate inertia, as if there was in us a need for oblivion and unconsciousness? In our willingness to let others assume our power, we look to them to define us and our role in society, and to provide us with a sense of who we are, thereby keeping ourselves detached from our essence. This self-alienation makes us afraid that our ignorance of our real selves might be exposed. This establishes a chasm between the beings we think we are and the beings we truly are, a chasm between thought and action, which drains the very energy that we need to live our everyday lives. It brings about fear of the future and other such mental projections as hope and belief systems, which effect our attitude towards disease, ageing and death. One can catch death just as one catches a cold: the process is the same.

Conflict and fragmentation provide the hooks by means of which germs, toxins or viruses attach themselves to an organ, instead of simply passing through the human body. Mental projections uses up a lot of energy that could be employed in keeping the regulatory mechanisms alive and functioning well. The bonding of energy through gravitational attraction has had such a strong effect on consciousness that it has allowed the rational thought process and reason to create a dichotomy between the feeling or the thought of who we are and our essential being. It is this ordinary subjective consciousness that cultivates and gives precedence to the laws operating in time, space and matter. Is it possible to get out of this situation? What can be done? Is it possible to loosen the bars of the prisons of time, space and matter, and to transmute the mental, emotional and physical blocks that prevent us from fully experiencing who we truly are? Now, the moment has come, until such time as we know directly, to trust the inherent intelligence of life itself to bring us the understanding of our true self and of the world.

The direct perception of the light that is the fabric of matter without any limits is possible through the principle of insight/illumination. Perception, attention, silence, natural tranquillity and intuition are some of the means by which we can gain an understanding of the nature of this principle, which then take us from the subconscious shores of the marshes of the savannah to the light that the awakened objective consciousness with its ability to de-crystallise the frozen light that matter is reveals in these very shores. No pollution can withstand that light, no projection can reach it, no assumption can pervert it. It is sufficient simply to abide in our own truth and to remain there as light proclaims further truths, simpler in their singularity.

In the words of Krishnamurti, "What is the action which is self-energising? An action which is infinite movement with infinite energy? Is there any action which is not of time? ... A way of living which is action in which there is no conflict? ... An action which is without friction... Is there an action which is a movement out of time?"[52]

There is such an action and it is attention with the extended meaning of being totally with the object of one's attention. What is attention? It is the interplay of two aspects of our being: perception and consciousness. What is perception? A cockerel is crowing. That is the fact. With its throat it is creating a sound wave in space. This hits your ear, interacting with the energy coming from your ear and activating within it certain elements that allow the sound to be heard. It is a purely mechanical process that the hen experiences as well. She does not say: "I hear the cockerel!" "I" cannot hear, it is the ears that hear. So in true perception, there is no ego, no "I". The hen will respond automatically to the call of the cockerel. At the animal level, cockerel and hen will perceive and know directly but without knowing that they know.

The second aspect of attention is concerned with consciousness. What is consciousness? It is a vibration that is a combination of light and sound but not yet manifest. I was struck by the phrase consciousness is its content, which can be turned around and expressed thus: the content of consciousness is consciousness. Let us consider a river which consists of flowing water. If we take the content of the river, the flowing water, away is there any river? Consciousness always has an object at the level of perception at which we agree to function. I call this subjective consciousness. Remove the object there is no perception, no consciousness. And yet there is something, which I call objective consciousness, no longer defined by an object. It is pure vibration. So in consciousness, there is no ego, no "I". In both perception and consciousness, the absence of ego means that there is nothing to appropriate the energies of the facts.

Attention is perception in action, indeed it is action. That action produces its own endless energy, without conflict, without friction, and is a movement out of time, space and matter. It is the light forever renewing itself, with no cause, no beginning and no ending.

"In that attention there is no going after, there is no wiping away. From that attention, observation, belief ends in me, not in you. It ends. In that attention, I see that any form of conformity breeds fear, suppression, obedience. So, in that very attention, I wipe that away in me, and any action based on reward or punishment is out, finished. So, what has happened? I see that any action in relationship, based on an image divides people. In paying attention to the known, all the factors of the known, their structure and their nature end. And then attention becomes very important. Attention says: "Is there any action which has none of these things?

M: Would you say that attention itself has none of these things?

A: Would you say that attention itself is action?

K: That is it. Therefore, attention is perception in action and therefore in that there is no conflict. It is infinite. The action of a belief is wastage of energy. Action in attention is producing its own energy and it is endless. The brain has functioned always in the field of conflict, belief, imitation, conformity obedience, suppression; it has always functioned that way and when the brain begins to know that, then attention begins to work. The brain cells themselves become attentive..." and later, Krishnamurti tells us again:

"...When there is complete attention, right inside, not imposed, not directed not willed, then the whole structure is alive, not in the usual sense, but in a different sense. I think there is a physical transformation. I think it is a direction of death and death is that. So, there is an action which is non-repetitive and therefore freedom from the known is attention in the unknown."[53]

In another context, we find this precision: "Specific information for each and every situation is being supplied to you constantly by the source of infinite knowledge. Why not trust it? Your first impulse will always be, as it has always been, the programmatic instruction from your subliminal analysis system, the advice of your Creator. It will be a direct message from your true self, the impulse of Life, the gateway to all that you call heaven. It is the spontaneous spark of divinity as it differentiates through you into your environmental situation. It can assess and evaluate the factors present in any situation at a rate of speed far exceeding a rational thought process. You have all the pertinent information in the universe available simply for the asking.

When you are aware of your totality, the Life-impulse will transmit to you everything that you need to know in any given situation. Its message will always come as your first spontaneous impulse. Be attentive."[54]

The language of light can be heard when there is silence. Not the silence which is simply the absence of external sounds, but the silence that arises spontaneously from the very depth of our being, a dynamic yet steady state of natural tranquillity. At such moments it is the energy itself that manifests its own way of release and of transformation, guided, as it were, by the basic intuitive faculties that work towards the fulfilment of the highest potential of the forms that they inhabit. And to quote Krishnamurti again: "There is an energy which is renewing itself all the time, which is not mechanistic, which has no cause, which has no beginning and therefore no ending. It is an eternal movement."

That energy in form is simply light, light that is renewing itself all the time. Light is the fuel, the force that animates the form. It is the core of every being, of every entity and this is why from our standpoint as beings of light, we are in a universe of equals, all part of the same essence. From that standpoint, there is no authority, no comparison, no greater or lesser. It is why it is important that we be a light unto ourselves, because that light contains all knowledge, from the atomic level to the cosmic level. We can now recognise the importance of heeding Polonius's injunction to Laertes in "Hamlet": "To thine own self be true: and it must follow as the night the day Thou canst not then be false to any man. "

An atom is a particle of light as well as a cell. This opens up tremendous possibilities. It becomes then a question of simply listening in or attending to what the cells are saying beyond their fears, their little mental projections and the habits which they have maintained for millions of years. And the cells say "I am whole." Behind the illusory veil that the mind is busy preserving, there is a realm of creativity where disease, accidents, ageing and death simply cannot be that is constantly concealed from our perception and our attention. This is the energy, the light, beyond all restraints of time and space, beyond matter, beyond duality, beyond specific purposes.

What can we do? If light reveals who we truly are, and if that light is the core of each cell, it means that encoded within each cell is the information that it needs to realise itself. This is the blueprint for biological fulfilment at the cellular level. The cells of the body can ignite themselves from inside and fuelled by the wind of spirit they can awaken and repair the dormant or diseased cells so that the fire can spread throughout the whole of the body. We seem to be coming to a time when this can be contemplated and the arteries flowing with light and life will spread from the body through to the earth with its lines of energy. The cell in a body of light is light itself. Like a hologram, a cell in the body is a cell of the whole. Indeed it is the whole. If we are to pray, why not pray to a cell in the liver?

"... Each healthy cell knows itself in essence as indistinguishable from its Creator. Just as the genetic code, with the complete design of the entire body spelled out in micro-detail, is contained in each cell of the human body, so contained within each human being is the complete blueprint for this entire universe and for the whole body that shall soon clothe its Creator."[55]

The experience of "the Mother" in Pondicherry beautifully illustrates this; it is described thus: "I have had a unique experience. Supramental light entered my body directly, without passing through states of consciousness, inner or higher. It was the first time and it came in through the feet...I saw a marvellous, warm, intense red and gold colour. And it was going up, it was going up indeed. And while it was going up, the fever started too because my body was not used to this intensity. When all this light reached my head, I thought I was going to burst and that I should stop the experience. Then, very clearly, I received the instructions to let serenity and peace descend on me and to expand my body consciousness, all my cells so that they could contain supramental light. I then found myself in another world...

...Another world, but not too far away. This world was almost as substantial as the physical world. There were bedrooms — Sri Aurobindo's bedroom with his bed — and he lived there: it was his home. There was even my bedroom with a large mirror, like the one I have here, there were combs and all sorts of things. And these objects were substantially almost as dense as in the physical world, but they were radiating their own light: it was not translucid, transparent, nor shining but light in itself. The objects, the bedrooms' matter did not have the opacity of physical objects, they were not dry and hard as in the physical world.

... And when I woke up I did not have this usual feeling of returning from far and that I needed to re-enter my body. No, it was simply as if I were in this other world, took a step back and I found myself here. It took me a good half hour to understand that our world does exist as much as the other one, that I was not on the other side, but here in the world of lies. I had forgotten everything: people, things, what I had to do — everything had vanished just as if it was not real. Indeed, we do not need to create this world of truth from scratch: it is ready, it is here, just like a copy of ours. Everything is there. EVERYTHING is there.

... I stayed there two complete days, two days of absolute bliss. And Sri Aurobindo was with me all the time: when I walked, he walked by me; when I sat down, he sat down next to me. At the end of the second day however, I realised that I could not stay there because work was not progressing. One has to do one's work in matter - to realise ourselves has to be done here, in this physical world otherwise we are not complete. So I withdrew and started to work again."[56]

This description gives a hint of the different levels at which life is possible for us to perceive reality. The fire of illumination is only waiting to rise phoenix-like from the ashes of all the materialising influences which surround us, and to sing, from the depth of each cell the song of insight and love, the song of unity.

Let us borrow the words of Rodney Collin to describe the principle of insight/illumination as being "the lightning flash in which all is timelessly created, revealed, absorbed." It echoes the saying in the prophecies that "the lightning that lighteth one particle that was bound on the heaven, shinest forth and lighteth another part on the heaven."

SUMMARY

The creative impulse in the light-mind of the Designer produces a cosmos, what we perceive as a material universe. In that process it somehow seems to lose its source-nature: the universe appears to be gross, dense, impermeable, dark: especially in the dark moments of our personal or collective history. The Buddha and other great teachers acted as catalysts for a reversal of this process in consciousness: the ascent "from the unreal to the real, from darkness to light, from death to immortality".

But, are not most of us trapped in materialism, repetition, and self-destructive habits? Are we not facing individual and global suicide? How can we ever break free of the world, if our energies are themselves worldly?

I propose that dynamics or principles from the transcendent dimension need our sincere attention. First we need to acknowledge them, then they will accommodate us.

Attention has qualities that we often miss. Deep, penetrating attention "sees" and it also "acts". When attention focuses with sufficient intensity, it produces an effect on the object of attention. Intensity is generated only if we dispense with artifice, evasion, and rigidity.

If we are attentive to our inner being, with intensity, we receive information in transmissions from the Light-impulse. This information is always perfectly suited to whatever situation we may encounter.

Our structures may appear to be materially based, but we are in essence creatures of light. Light pervades the entire cosmos. The cells of our body have a core of light. The principle of illumination refers to the unveiling of this reality.

True insight reveals the nature of the light at the core of the cells and the same light at the core of consciousness and the universe. In a human being, cells may reveal their light in spontaneous bursts spreading through and outside the body. This process embodies the fulfilment of human potential at a biological level.

CHAPTER NINE

THE
PRINCIPLE
OF
COMMUNION/
COMMUNICATION

Seek beauty and you find
a taste of love
Find love and you commune
with oneness

As the universe expands, principles that were in potential are actualised and the forces that they generate help us to incarnate principles which still remain in potential within us. The last two principles are those of insight/illumination and of communication/communion. The former, as we discussed, was ushered in on the current of the Buddhic energy and the latter, whose wave is now breaking on the shores of our being, by the Christ energy. The principle of communication/communion is firmly rooted in a love that is now bringing to the One Home all the harvests of the last few million years.

The essence of love is expressed in the principle of communication/ communion and the historical Jesus was the herald of the awakening in time, space and matter of the energy of that principle which operates in the timeless, the spaceless and the formless. The Christ energy served as a catalyst in the actualisation of the blueprint of objective love.

I wish to make it clear that when I speak of Gautama and Jesus, I refer to specific historical characters and not to archetypal forms of energy. Through their actions and their words during their stay on earth, these figures were able to convey an understanding of specific forms of vibration - the Buddhic and the Christic, - which they seem to have embodied. They reduced the diversity of belief systems and the manifold existential quests of their time to a simple teaching that made its mark in the consciousness of people with an impact that we can still feel today, two and a half thousand and two thousand years after their respective departures from this Earth. Other people may have embodied such extraordinary vibrations but they are lost in history.

The principles clothe these vibrations in such a way that their intrinsic qualities and values are accentuated. I hope that their presentation and discussion in this book will make them more accessible to our understanding, thereby accelerating their integration into our lives. It is vital that this should happen for we seem to have very little time left before an extraordinary shift occurs, a paradigm change in which we are the players, the spectators and the composers. Better learn our parts well than stumble on to the stage unrehearsed. The song to learn is short: "Thou shalt love the Lord thy God with all thy heart, and with all thy soul, and with all thy mind....Thou shalt love thy neighbour as thyself."[57]

The principle of communication/communion is the ultimate energy of which we can be aware from the standpoint of our limited consciousness that operates in time, space and matter. The law that derives from it is the supreme regulation that both we and the universe can appreciate: objective love. The wonder of it is that, although it operates out of time, space and matter, we can feel its effects here and now which is why, with our limited means, we are able to perceive its essence and partake of it.

In fact, we perceive who we are. At least, we perceive what our means of perception are. If I look at you, I see the fact of you. If I look at you through a microscope I see another fact of you, but each fact is true according to whichever way I look at you. If my means of perception are refined, then I perceive finer matter. If I have the ability to see energy fields, then I perceive you as a shimmer of light with more or less "density". In that context, what I perceive is in accordance to the setting to which I adjust my perception. Could we perhaps say that the perceiver is the perceived in the same way that beauty is in the eye of the beholder?

There is a headache. I give it total attention, without concentration. A light, almost tender perception is in play. There is no longer any notion of time as the attention seems to bore more deeply into the pain. First the pain is enhanced but then it lightens and suddenly there is a burst of light and energy. The pain has vanished. What has happened is that the pain has revealed its truth: it is nothing more than a manifestation of energy, a convergence of forces that has dissolved through attention. This is the way in which attention is action. Apply this attention to all manifestations of life and events of this nature may well occur. Therein lies communication.

What is it that one is communicating with? Nothing other than oneself. True communication occurs when the I or the ego is absent, when the illusory concentration of power, which is all that it is, no longer finds any support in activities that it claims it performs, and when the thought forms that it engenders receive no energy from its self centred use of intelligence. Indeed how can it be said that I hear or that I eat? The ears hear, the mouth masticates the food and the digestive juices process it. Where is the "I" in all these processes? Once these processes are seen for what they are, then communication can arise, with each separate level of organisation being responsible for its own type of communication. It is, in fact, impossible to communicate *with*, (only the "I" or ego can do that); what actually happens is communion.

With the disappearance of the ego, then there is no separation, the observer being the observed, consciousness being consciousness of itself, with no so-called external or internal object. It is simply consciousness observing. Whether it is consciousness of an atom or of a human being, or of a galaxy, consciousness in the process of observing is nothing other than the actual power of the fact. In other words, consciousness acting as power is communication. Or the action of consciousness and power is communication. This is implicit in Jesus' words to his disciples: "I tell you solemnly, if your faith were the size of a mustard seed, you could say to this mountain: 'Move from here to there,' and it would move; nothing would be impossible for you."[58]

Your friend, an artist, has sent you her latest painting as a present, warning you that it is not quite finished, but wanting you to have it in time for your birthday. On the morning, you unwrap the gift that turns out to be a magnificent representation of the glade where you like to walk. With her inspiration your friend has managed to capture a particular quality of the light that attracts you to the place. Light suffuses the whole painting. The quality of the rendition overwhelms you. You notice the unfinished spot. Though your joy is renewed each time you look at the painting or even just think about it, still the unfinished spot keeps on niggling you. You decide to do something about it yourself, so you research the right pigment and the right brush, and with a good deal of concentration, application and practice, you manage to approximate the mood of the whole painting and to complete the masterpiece. This is the ridiculous way which we are accustomed to proceed, and it has validity if we are stubborn enough to keep on being thoroughly involved with the domain of matter which has a duration in time and occupies a position in space. Can there be another way?

Let us imagine that the present of the painting which is given to you on your birthday is, instead, the living present of you to yourself. You, the painting, are a fact, a specific convergence of forces at a specific level, while the unfinished part of the painting is another convergence of forces, still you but at a slightly different level of organisation. The piece of blank canvas may be compared to a blockage of energy, which can manifest as a disease, a spasm in a muscle, or a headache. These too are a convergence of forces but they are not necessarily in harmony with the surrounding environment. Different levels with different organisations. You are attentive to the facts, acknowledge their presence and let them be. In detachment thus expressed, a matrix is created, which contains two elements: power and consciousness. The power is the energy of the facts, the consciousness stems from the attention. An alchemical action takes place. In the crucible of objective love that is the matrix, there is an instantaneous dissolution and commingling of all the facts, the whole of you including the energy blockage, a global event that happens out of time, light communing with light and organising itself to form a greater or finer structure. Your painting has finished itself.

In a dark room, a light is switched on and at once light bathes the whole of the room and all the objects in it, be they ugly, beautiful, bulky, or refined. There is no differentiation. That is communication.

We usually approach everything from the standpoint of effort and duality, because we are so keen to allow the laws operating in time, space, matter and mind to bind us: you and me, subject and object, all the degrees between the poles. This is also the world of emotion where objective love has no place. Faced with the naked power of life, the gaol of matter is so secure! And we are constantly sabotaging our means of integrating into ourselves the power with which we invest matter.

The group of therapists that met that day discovered that there was a state of conflict between two of them. The situation had come to a head. All the members of the group were aware that the whole thing had to come out into the open. The therapeutic model with which the therapists work got into place and there was the feeling of a tremendous violence. It was not possible to leave the situation as it was; it had to be resolved. Consequently time had to be put aside for discussion and for management of the conflict, thus establishing the conflict in its own right, and giving it energy. For things to proceed, there would have to be a facilitator and of course there would be the games of power and control going on. Not all the members of the group were free then, so another meeting was arranged for later in the day.

Confrontation was the wave of the moment and everybody was busy establishing the parameters wherein it could flow. Could there be a wave without beaches, a wave in communion with the ocean?

The two people who were in conflict stayed on and I joined them. I asked them to just look at the situation: "Is there anything to settle? You have already defined the conflict for yourselves. There is frustration, there is resentment, there is disappointment. These are the facts. The other person who creates this resentment has nothing to do with your resentment. It is your resentment, it is your fact and it is valid. Consider that fact like a baby that you hold in your arms and let it be because this manifestation of energy is infinitely precious. You are disappointed and that is your fact. So what are the facts? Emotional leftovers. You have defined one important fact in you and you can settle that in yourself by being attentive to it."

Suddenly they were given a tremendous concentration of energy through clear perception and attention to their facts, which were frustration, resentment, anger, feelings of worthlessness, disappointment, and so on. They started to get an inkling of the underlying patterns at work, and one of them recognised that the resolution of the conflict was not the issue. She saw that if resentment was the basic pattern, it would happen time and again if it was not attended to for what it was. People look outside for explanations, projecting their own facts onto others. They are not, however, resentful because of someone else. If it is their pattern to be resentful, then that is valid. In a way it is like dropping a pebble in the water. If people really did accept what was in them and did something about it, would not the ripples of energy go out to others? Once people see what is going on it can, however, be tempting to try and "work on" the situation.

Then you are back to square one, with the mind creating the programme to "work on it". There is still involvement in the specific movement of change. You can, like one of these therapists in conflict, want to change the resentment into no resentment, frustration into no frustration and so on. That is perfectly valid at the level of awareness at which they were both operating but that movement of change will happen only in time, space and matter and out of a basic need for comfort and maintaining the *status quo* going. This will not transform the underlying pattern. Only love can do that.

Facts are convergence of forces, sources of power. The feeling of frustration is a fact, an energy with a specific vibration. Attention is perception and consciousness, which in essence has no ego content, no mind content.

Consciousness is also a specific vibration. Attention brings the two waves of vibration together. The action of power and consciousness is communication. The marrying of the two waves of vibration is an act of objective love that transmutes the vibration of the initial fact into a finer vibration. Frustration therefore transforms into release and a clear flow of energy. Metamorphosis is the energetic transmutation of one level of expression into a finer one.

* * * * * * * * * *

The word emotion comes from the Latin *"ex-movere"*, meaning to move out. With emotions, what is one moving out of, if not one's centre? But then what is it in us that creates the idea of a centre if not the mind? If there is a centre, then there must be a periphery, and hence duality. In love, in unity, there is no centre, no door to open, no door to close.

When the lover says to the beloved: "I love you," that is an affirmation of duality, of polarity, of the fact that "I" is different from "you". There are two entities here, apparently bound together by love. This expression of emotion has nothing to do with communication. In fact, emotion excludes communication. It is however possible at times to experience communication from our standpoint in time, space and matter - watching the sunset, for example, or at times of unbearable pain. The emotion comes later, in the description of the event. Mystics and poets throughout the ages have been inspired to produce wonderful accounts of such experiences and to give us a taste of their rapture.

At our more earthly level, the two lovers may now and then experience a timelessness when their union becomes so refined that they dive into the unity that we essentially are. Their energies are as one. Their sense of self disappears then as their energies merge. A feeling of bliss is experienced, an oceanic feeling where we are transported by waves of vibration and energy. The energies are one. This is true communication. The state, for it is a state, can last for a long period but there is no notion of time, of space or of identity for the lovers.

It appears to be more common that only one of the lovers "knows" this state rather than the two of them entering the seemingly endless and timeless embrace at the same time. As soon as one of the partners "wakes up" (or should we say: "wakes down"!) and says to the other: "I love you," the communication ends because the mind is using the energy to express the emotion. In this context, spoken communication kills the communing. The state will linger for a while but is impossible to recapture, as that would involve a movement of energy towards repeating the experience, which that very movement would make impossible. Such an experience simply happens.

"If we translate the experience of sexuality onto the mental plane it becomes clear that the human longing for eternal happiness can only be stilled by a return to the unity from which we originally came. This ultimate fusion with the great all-embracing consciousness is the goal common to many different religions and esoteric systems, and a variety of images and terms are used to describe it:

211

the Chemical Wedding of the alchemists, the conjunction of opposites, the unio mystica, and so on."[59]

Communication is instantaneous because we communicate "with" ourselves. By being true to ourselves, we perceive *who* we are, and beyond that we can have an insight into *what* we are, the light covered by veils which attention dissolves, closing the gap between the perception and oneself. There is no otherness. Communication in this way does not mean exchange, which would imply duality. This means that there can be no intervention as everything is clearly seen as expressing the awareness and creating the reality that is right, perfect and necessary for that level.

You notice that there is a tree growing at an angle in the clearing to which your feet have lead you. Everything else is in perfect balance as you commune with the state of suspension that pervades the play of sunlight on leaves and moss. The sensuous dance of the ferns echoes the velvety swish of the birds' wings in the redolent air. The slight imperfection of a leaning tree wounds your sensitivity and so you decide to dedicate yourself to correcting this quirk of nature. Resolute, you erect scaffolding and with ropes, ever so gently, over a long period, you begin to pull the tree upright, hoping to restore it to its correct balanced position in the wood. One day, you surprise an elderly man sitting at the edge of the clearing. "What are you doing?" he asks. "Don't you see!" you exclaim. "I am restoring harmony." With a commanding voice he replies: "Look!" Through his eyes you see and feel the tellurian currents and fields of energy that made the tree grow and lean in perfect harmony with that other level of being.

Everything communicates, in harmony with the level of vibration at which it manifests, whatever that level may be. What is perceived may be there because the operation of one level of energy and consciousness makes it absolutely necessary that things should be the way they are on another level. We can therefore say with certainty that everything is perfect.

The keener the attention, the more communication and revelation of worlds upon worlds of manifestation there is. These worlds are nothing other than different aspects of ourselves, of the Self that the mind has contrived to limit to a body, a personality, an ego and an undue sense of self with a small "s". Noticing these facts, acknowledging their presence, agreeing to let them be and even to let go of the knowledge – detachment in other words – allows a tremendous respect and love to fuel this attention at deeper levels.

Another definition of detachment is a keen alertness to the facts and a constantly renewed willingness to let these facts be, because we recognise that the power of the facts is sufficient to transform them from within. Facts are nothing other than embodiments of truth and light. When facts - such as atoms, cells, organs of the body, pains, emotions, and ideas - move together with a common pulse, fulfilling at their own level their purpose, indeed the common purpose when these facts exists purely to realise their potential of light, truth and love, then an amazing force, an ecstatic rhythm takes over.

Each unit is a true individual (without division), united with the whole, moving as a single body, tracing out new forms and patterns and resorbing them in a dance of deep communion. Pure detachment allows all units to be poised. The mind at peace does not give direction to their energy which can act of its own accord, evolving its own transformation. The action happens without premeditation, choice or thought. When Christ said: "Thy Kingdom come on earth," he was pointing to the potential, at our level of existence, of an apotheosis of transformation. Resurrection is the essence of metamorphosis. It is possible because when the materialising influences stop exercising their hold, this seeming crucifixion puts an end to their divided state of the materialising influences.

At that level the mind keeps on wanting to exercise the tyranny of form whose entropy is habit. The state that allows us to break free from habit is the state of grace that is connected to the principle of communication/communion. While the state of bliss is a state of suspension beyond all direction and meaning, the state of grace is a fulfilment enshrined at the core of the body's cells at the physical level and other levels. It is a state of being held in the heart of life. The oneness is a ripe fruit.

"Beings who function in a state of grace are secure in the knowledge that conceptual understanding is there whenever they choose to slow into it, but they have released their addiction to the 'fruit of the tree of the knowledge of good and evil.' *They no longer require a symbolic interpretation of each moment.* Because of this, it sometimes appears to those observing through the old historical filters that those functioning in the new paradigm are ignoring common sense. But this is never the case.

The behaviour of those who function in a state of grace makes perfect sense, but it is sense that is drawn from a higher frequency of awareness. Its logic is not within ego's grasp, but it is of a more rapid vibration than the slower-frequency logic of the ego. For the ego to understand the lightning process through which the spirit reaches a sequence of decisions, it has to break down the process and study it one frame, one step at a time. While this can be done, it is much better to experience instinctual awareness than to analyse it"[60].

We commune with the whole universe which is nothing other than our own being. The finer worlds that we are, in order to bypass the machinations of the mind, will disguise their voice so as to make known their truth and enjoin us to reach and abide with them, which is to abide in the deeper levels of our own being. We do not need to reach for these levels because they are, in fact, the very essence of ourselves. If one were to seek them, then the road would lead away from what we truly are. However, when attention is present, these exquisite worlds also dissolve, fulfilling their destiny of releasing their light as the night closes around us and the void opens its arms.

The poet has defined communication/communion as the ultimate emotion of life and creation at the threshold of the manifest and the non-manifest. This principle belongs to the world of unity out of time, space, matter and form and it regulates the subtlest levels of the universe forever arising out of the fount of objective love. Ultimately, the order of the universe can be perceived only by love. "Love is the movement of beauty and beauty is the ultimate aim of Love."

SUMMARY

One experiences a burst of light and energy as the fact reveals itself, as the manifestation unfolds its meaning. In a sense, "I" am communicating with "it". But that level of communication still implies a duality.

We know from recent discoveries in physics, as well as from our mystical heritage, that there is no duality. The universe is a seamless whole with no division between subject and object. Moreover, the whole universe is ever in a state of communion with itself. There are no spatial, temporal, or material barriers to instantaneous communication throughout the cosmos.

When I meet the other - a person, an idea, a fact - who am I meeting? I am meeting myself.

As the bursts of energy and light multiply we appear to see deeper and deeper levels of manifestation. According to the principle of communication, these are also levels of ourselves.

From this perspective, the universe unfolds its drama with every element fulfilling its purpose at its own level, in its own sub-system. Everything is perfect.

There arises a sense that Love is built into the fabric. This Love is not the love for family or friends or lovers; human love can be a good pointer to the universal Love, but it may also become cloying and jealous. Love is a quality we can ascribe to the creative dimension, as we can also ascribe light, bliss, and intelligence. I consider this to be objective love.

Communion is achieved through an inner alchemy, a fusion of consciousness and the power of truth.

Communion is a state of grace. Yet it is not to be reached for or achieved. It is our own inner state, our birthright, our essence. It is realised after the release of all energies from their apparent bondage.

CHAPTER TEN

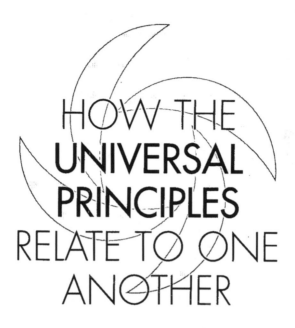

HOW THE
UNIVERSAL
PRINCIPLES
RELATE TO ONE
ANOTHER

Having considered the nine Universal Principles one by one, I now want to look at their effect on our lives today. I found that they encapsulate everything that I have observed in the course of my work with people over many years and so I decided to apply them systematically to my own life. Since then my everyday life has been a very thrilling adventure. Apparently random events started acquiring a meaning which had hitherto been missed because of the mind's refusal to have any truck with the wisdom of the heart.

Philosophical systems in the past have, for the most part relied on the dynamism of the law of causation to make sense of the mysteries of life, always seeking to understand the nature of the first Cause. Through the Principle of 'Causation the mind tries to ensure that this game of enquiry goes on forever, and that its appetite for control and power will continue to be assuaged. It will go on trying to bridge the gap between the different spheres of existence until it finds itself in a cul-de-sac and even the energy trapped there will provide the impetus for it to go on playing the game on slightly different fields. After all, isn't that the way of evolution?

Causation, we now know, is at play within one and only one sphere of existence and activity. It cannot link or be used to bridge two or more spheres. Let us go back to our previous example of the growth of a seed. Two things happen: the seed comes into contact with the earth and with moisture which combine to open up its outer covering; the life within the seed transforms it. The mind would like to say that it is the work of earth and water which causes the plant to grow, choosing to ignore that there are two distinct spheres of activity, denying the truth. Causation is at work within one sphere: it is only because the seed is alive that it grows into a plant. Earth and water will open up the outer covering of a dead seed. It, however, will turn into humus and enrich the earth. There will be no plant.

Though the Principle of Causation may have played a small role in our understanding of the nature of the Universal Principles and of how they interact, its logic pales into insignificance when we consider the logic of the Principle of Correspondences which is the basis of this book. That is why, in this chapter, I will not be directly addressing the question of *why* things are as they are when I describe how I have found the principles to interrelate. This book and the work described in it have come about, at one level, through observation, experience, reasoning, and logic, and, at another level, out of intuition, insight and infused knowledge, allowing for layer upon layer of 'knowing' to reveal itself. Not meeting the linear demands of the mind accustomed to the milk of causation may cause frustration but this weaning ensures, as far as I am concerned, the integration of a much richer and more sustaining food with which the expanding *or* developing consciousness of humanity may nourish itself – universal rather than linear. Questioning all our fixed assumptions and starting from zero can allow us a much wider insight into reality than if we remain within the field of causation and duality. The exploration and explanation of the process of discovery may give an understanding of how my mind works, but the underlying dynamism stems from a movement of being which is firmly grounded in the field of unity. Indeed it is our privilege, as human beings, to be able to be conscious of that field at the same time as we can perceive that we also belong - albeit secondarily - to the field of duality.

If everything reflects every other thing, as the principle of correspondence teaches us that it does, then it follows that the principles would be reflected in different parts of the body. Observation and logic have shown me that this is, in fact, the case and I have been able to discover the specific points on the feet, hands and head that relate to the different principles. This enables us to gain a greater insight into the relationships of the universal principles with one another and with the human body, given that the principles are reflected in different areas of the body, which are in their turn reflected in specific points on the feet, hands and head.

The sexual organs are used to "cause" a new life and consequently the principle of causation is reflected in the genital area of the body. For reproduction to take place, it requires two partners of opposite sex. Males and females are both cut from the same cloth, which is composed of two aspects, the masculine and the feminine. We know this from the principle of gender, which I found reflected in the base of the spine. The new manifestation, the new being, will eventually open out to the world and this will be reflected at the level of the solar plexus which in the Metamorphic Technique's prenatal pattern does indeed correspond to the opening to the world and this is where the principle of correspondence is situated. "As within, so without, as above, so below". Breathing, with the chest rising and falling, gives a very good illustration of the movement from one pole to the other and the principle of rhythm is indeed reflected in the chest. This leaves the one principle which is still operating in duality, that of polarity. Looking again at the prenatal pattern which is reflected along the spine, with the moment of conception reflected at the atlas or first cervical vertebra and the moment of birth reflected at the coccyx, there was one area left, the throat. I consider the throat to be the umbilical cord between the cosmos and the earth, and this mirrors the two poles of the principle of polarity. These five principles, of gender, causation, correspondence, rhythm and polarity are at work in the domain of time, space and matter, the domain of duality.

A totally non-physical aspect of our life is registered in the pineal gland whose function is very much concerned with light and the principle of creative impulse is indeed reflected there. As the master gland of the endocrine system, the pituitary gland relates to 'higher mind' interpreting the light of creation and putting it into a form that is comprehensible to the human mind. It reflects a form of consciousness that is about to become finite and relates to the principle of vibration which also fulfils that role. These two principles are at work in the domain out of time, space and matter, the domain of unity.

At a certain stage in my exploration I was aware of only the first seven principles, of which The Kybalion spoke. I felt, however, that they fell into three groups which I now call triads. The first triad includes the principles of gender, causation and correspondence which are connected with the lower part of the body up to the diaphragm. The second triad is made up of the principles of rhythm, polarity and vibration and these are related to the upper part of the body, including the pituitary gland.

Why should the principle of vibration, whose essence belongs to the domain out of time, space and matter, be included in this second triad? The first, or base, triad is common to both animals and humans. However, the fact that humans are self-reflective, that we are aware that we are aware, distinguishes us from animals in that we realise that we are more than our purely animal instincts and our self-gratifying drive, and that we can understand the meaning of innocence, compassion and love. The principle of vibration, we have seen, is in the ratio of the contraction to expansion. Through contraction, energy is saved which may then be used for expansion or the discovery of subtler levels of being, which will be expressed in time, space and matter through polarity and rhythm which has its own momentum.

That left the principle of creative impulse, which is connected with the pineal gland. In the same way as a dream takes place in a moment of time and ends with the stimulus that started it, so a new life is focused on or in, the pineal, which has not been created yet, but which is nevertheless the focal point. The focal point for what? This question triggered off a deeper exploration of the nature of the principles.

Why would there be one principle on its own, whereas the other two groups had three each? Something was missing. When I was giving seminars on my understanding of the universal principles at that time, and we came to discuss the way they related to one another I would insert question marks for the two principles I felt were missing. Why had the authors of the "Kybalion", presenting some of Hermes's work on the Universal Principles, not mentioned them? Could it have been that at that time in ancient Egypt, the energies of these two principles were not yet activated, potentially present but imperceptible to the subjective consciousness of the time?

I have been told of examples of such consciousness-blindness. It seems that when the Spaniards first arrived on the coast of South America, the natives thought they must be gods descended from the heavens. Oral tradition had informed them of such a possible occurrence but apparently they could not understand how these people had been able to reach their shores in the small boats that were drawn up on the beach. The large sailing boats with their alien construction were only really seen properly when the natives boarded them. Could Hermes have suffered from a similar consciousness-blindness with the two 'missing' principles, which even though they existed in potential in human consciousness only became actualised much later?

Over the years, I had come to the conclusion that five of the principles were connected with time, space and matter and that the other two, which I had verified, were operating out of time, space and matter but nevertheless affecting us here and now. During a seminar attended by four men and three women, the nature of the further two "missing" principles became apparent: they were the principles of insight and of communication. The group's magnetic energy had drawn to us, as with the principle of creative impulse, the fine energy of these two other principles, triggering in us the knowledge of their nature. However, subsequently, it became evident that these two words alone were not describing entirely the nature of the energies of the two principles which I had picked up. Certain aspects were missing. Insight and communication were seemingly the masculine qualities of these two principles, but later the feminine qualities were revealed as illumination and communion. As these two principles belonged entirely to the realm of the timeless, spaceless and formless, being suprahuman they did not have any point of reflection in the body. Strangely, however, there seemed to be both feminine and masculine aspects present in their nature, which I sense is probably due to our perceiving them through the filter of our own subjective consciousness. To further our understanding of the last two principles, I have added the word "revelation" to the principle of insight/illumination, and the word "harmony" to the principle of communication/communion.

How did these principles arise? We know that Zarathustra could feel the energy field that coalesced into objects, and that he spoke of this as the spirit that manifested to him in the form of light. As he recognised the actualisation of the principle of creative impulse in the consciousness of humans, he heralded the advent of the Buddhic energy field the essence of which is light. In his turn, through his being, his action and his compassion, the Buddha was the precursor of the teaching of Christ, which is embodied in the injunction: "Love Thy Neighbour as you love Thyself". The Christ energy field ushered in the principle of communication/communion and the ultimate self-sacrifice allowed the understanding of unity and the immanence of the "I AM" nature of Life within each of us to arise out of the shadow of matter. "My father and I are one and you are one with my father." Unity is also at the core of the Islamic teaching, the unity of creator and creation, with human beings serving as the connecting link between these two through self-reflective consciousness.

The actualisation of these last two principles happened at a point in history, which in the relative time frame of the evolution of the world, was no more than a minute ago, and therefore no specific physical organ had had time to develop to reflect them. Furthermore considering them obliges us to forget isolated parts in order to concentrate on the whole, which is entirely reflected in the parts. Not just one cell but an individual, not just an individual but the body of humanity, not just the body of humanity but the corpus of the cosmos and of all its units, light beings that are as many rays of the One light.

The first triad, or group of three principles, is concerned solely with the domain in time, space and matter, being reflected in the lower part of the body. The second triad contains the principles of Rhythm and Polarity which are also connected with time, space and matter and are reflected in the chest and the throat areas respectively, while it also contains the Principle of Vibration which is connected with the pituitary gland in the head, and the domain out of time, space and matter. The third triad is solely concerned with principles out of time, space and matter, even though the principle of creative impulse is reflected in the pineal gland. The other two principles in this triad are supra-human.

The dividing line between the bottom first and second triads is reflected in the diaphragm. The dividing line between the second and third triads is between the pituitary and the pineal gland in the body. One evening a woman from Germany who was on her way to New York to open a meditation centre came to one of my evening classes in London. At the end of the session she stayed on to share what she had noticed and told me that she had been disturbed by two important things that she had witnessed. "I can see the colours of the aura", she said, "and when people started working on each other's feet, the colour of the aura of the patient became violet and the colour of the aura of the practitioner became green". - "What is disturbing about that?" I asked. "You see, it doesn't fit in at all with my knowledge of the colour system because the practitioner giving healing is normally surrounded by a violet colour and the patient is surrounded by a green colour, the colour of the heart. I don't understand why it was reversed here tonight". - "This is a wonderful confirmation of the work", I told her, "because the practitioner is not attempting to give anything whatsoever to the person with whom she or he is working. Detachment is a deep expression of love and according to your system love is connected with the colour green. It is the energy of the patient that does the healing, hence the violet colour". She then added: "There is another thing that I am often aware of. I see inside people; a type of X-ray seeing. Teaching intensive meditation, at times I notice that the pineal gland glows slightly. But tonight, what happened was extraordinary because not only the pineal gland but also the pituitary gland became filled with light. The two glands were lit up and there was a bridge of light between them. I could see that bridge of light between the two foci of light, between the pineal and the pituitary glands". Later on I realised that this bridge of light may well play a specific function in our ability to establish a distinction between ethereal realms.

What the two glands represent is something that is out of time, space and matter. The pituitary gland, however, connects more closely with the dimension of matter, time and space in its function as the master gland of the endocrine system while the pineal gland is in close resonance with the domain of light and inspiration. In the same way, the physical drawing of the design is closer to the realisation and the actualisation of the piece of furniture than the thought of the designer is. At what moment does the precipitation in time, space and matter happen for a human being?

At conception, the genes of the first cell provide the structures of the past that attract the non-material influences that have an affinity with this new existence. This cell is not only a new type of organisation but much more importantly, a manifestation of the life and the intelligence whose vibration slows down in order to incarnate.

There are therefore three triads, one of which is more concerned with matter, time and space, while the other two regulate a finer quality of energy. Let us compare the first one to ice, the second to water, and the third to steam. If we consider ice, water and steam, we realise that they are of course made up of the same basic elements of hydrogen and oxygen but that different laws are more active for each of these three states. The important thing to remember is the underlying factor of H_2O.

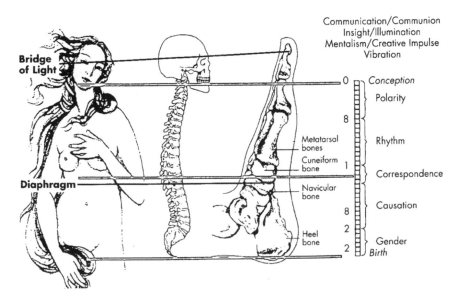

Chart of the Universal Principles as formulated by Gaston Saint-Pierre

We find then that we have three groups of triads with two dividing lines between them.

Reflexology has shown us that the spinal column is reflected on the bony ridge on the inside of the feet. The meeting point between the atlas and the base of the skull is mirrored on the side of the first articulation of the big toe. It has recently been discovered that the spinal reflex points also reflect specific moments of a person's gestation, from conception to birth. The moment of our conception is reflected at the first articulation of the big toe. (See a further explanation of this in "The Metamorphic Technique")[61]

Conception is where we start from, our reference point. It is at that moment that the universal principles order the progression of our presence in the world. The undifferentiated light, an idea in gestation on the brink of form and matter, takes on the elements that will colour its purity when, as a new being, it evolves in manifestation. Our purpose, and realisation of it, provide the direction for our evolution, not genetic mutation. By touching the point of conception we attune to the fundamental harmonies of the universe.

Of the nine principles that regulate the universe, its movement and the movements of everything in it, five of them operate in time, space and matter – the principles of gender, causation, correspondence, rhythm and polarity – while four of them operate out of time, space and matter – the principles of vibration, creative impulse, insight/illumination and communication/communion. Through further observation I have found that certain principles relate to others in a specific way, which gives us another three groupings which are different from those we called the triads:

1. Gender, Rhythm, Creative impulse
2. Causation, Polarity, Insight/Illumination
3. Correspondence, Vibration, Communication / Communion

This discovery, which is connected with the actual nature of the principles, was that some of them are a reflection of others at primary or higher levels.

The relationships between this second classification of the principles resemble those between the angles of a triangle. Let us therefore refer to them as the three triangles.

I found that there was a dynamic relationship between the three principles of insight/illumination, polarity and causation. The principle of insight/illumination is an expression of the essence of light which is reflected at lesser levels in the other two.

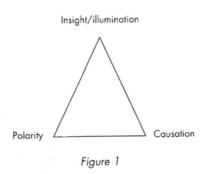

Insight/illumination

Polarity   Causation

Figure 1

The seat of the principle of polarity in the human body is at the level of the throat. Polarity is reflected at a grosser level of vibration in the principle of causation and in turn is the reflection of the principle of insight/illumination. The genitals "cause" the human being; through the throat, we "cause" words and the principle of insight/illumination is the spark for the flash of inspiration. These three principles are in a subtle relationship of degrees, the principle of polarity playing the middle role.

In the body the principle of causation has its seat of influence and manifestation in the lower part, in the genital area. It is the pale reflection of the principle that is located at the throat level, the principle of polarity, which influences us in such a way that we create our reality by attracting everything in our lives to us. Through the throat centre, we "cause," we create, by means of words. This again is a pale reflection of that much finer principle, the principle of insight/illumination, whereby a flash of lightning strikes, as it were, awakening us and allowing different perceptions and realisations at a level way beyond that of ordinary perception, knowledge, and understanding.

The principle of communication/communion, being an expression of the essence of love, is part of the dynamism which exists within the triangle where the two other angles are occupied by the principles of vibration and correspondence, both pale reflections at specific levels of the principle of communication/communion.

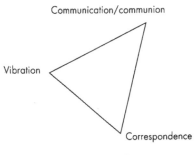

Figure 2

The principle of correspondence, reflected at the level of the solar plexus, brings in, in time, space and matter, a person's realisation of their autonomy, as they open up to the world and discover the realms of self and no-self. Out of time, space and matter, the principle of vibration expresses the actualisation of the creative impulse; it is reflected in the pituitary gland that acts as translator between the subtle and the physical realms - a place of rest for the visitor of subtle energies on the threshold of the manifest. It, in turn, is connected with the principle of communication/communion that affirms the unity of all living entities, being the ultimate emotion of life on the threshold between the manifest and the unmanifest.

As all living beings are an expression of an expansion/contraction ratio, and are vibrations at a specific frequency, then communication can be inferred as taking place at a finer level than that particular level of vibration. Indeed it is because there is communication/communion, or objective love, that vibration can arise at a grosser level which in the realm of time, space, and matter becomes correspondence. While still at the level out of time, space and matter and with the same dynamism, the law of communication/communion expresses itself as the principle of vibration, as the dimensions of matter, time and space are about to appear. As this last level manifests, the inherent dynamism gives rise to the principle of correspondence. In other words, communication becomes vibration becomes correspondence – the same dynamism but at different levels of expression.

The movement of the principle of Vibration reflected in the pituitary gland, is in its turn being established more specifically in the lower part of the body, from the solar plexus downward. The enzymes produced by the pituitary gland and those produced by the gonads are similar in nature, the former regulating the amount of pain that we can endure and the latter, our experience of pleasure. There is therefore a parallel between what happens in the realm out of time, space and matter at the level of vibration and the last four-and-a-half months of gestation. The tendencies established then constitute the feminine aspect of our being, our social outlook, and involvement with other people; this energy will be concerned with physical pursuits, and the ability to respond to what we become aware of, with activities rather than with thoughts.

The principle of creative impulse is related to the principle of rhythm which, in its turn, relates to the principle of gender. Or, looking at it from the lowest levels upwards, gender reflects the principle of rhythm, which in turn reflects the principle of creative impulse. This means that everything that exists can call upon the energies in the level above it, in order to achieve a state of equilibrium. For example, if the two poles, the masculine/feminine, in the principle of gender are well established in their own right, there can arise a subtle exchange of energy which creates a fine oscillation that could be compared to the principle of rhythm. An even more refined energy is the thought that lies behind manifestation. Such thoughts and ideas have their origin in consciousness, and consciousness in its turn has its origin in intelligence. So we can say that the principle of gender has its source in intelligence, and ultimately in the highest power there is, – Life. Life and intelligence, moving down through the levels to the lowest, manifest as gender, the first shaping law at the root of our essence or greater Self.

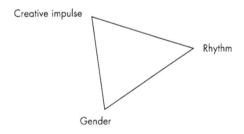

Creative impulse

Rhythm

Gender

Figure 3

The third triangle comprises the principle of creative impulse, the principle of gender and the principle of rhythm. At a basic level, the principle of gender suggests the coming together of pairs of opposites, active and receptive, light and dark, masculine and feminine. The principle of rhythm expresses the movement from one pole to another while the principle of creative impulse establishes the universe as idea at a subtler level of vibrations.

The light of the creative impulse, reflected in the pineal gland, establishes specific characteristics in the depths of our being during the post-conception period, approximately the first four and a half months. The tendencies which come in at that point constitute the masculine aspect of our being, our individualistic outlook, and involvement with self; this energy will be concerned chiefly with mental pursuits, the ability to be aware, perceiving the patterns without, however, becoming involved with them.

The principle of rhythm is reflected in the chest area of the body, while the principle of correspondence is reflected at the level of the solar plexus. We can compare the solar plexus to the hearth where the burning logs of a fire extend their flames up towards the heart where they start radiating as light.

These principles and the laws that derive from them regulate every fibre of our being, which means that we have no need to search for meaning, light or love but simply to realise that that is what we are. The quests, the seeking, the enlightenment programmes are devious devices which the mind employs to make sure that it retains control and that enlightenment is never realised. In some way, we are like a ball of wax, a network of converging forces whose vibrations have a fairly slow movement. Our ability to be aware that we are aware implies a faster rate of vibrations, which allows us to have an overview of these converging forces. However, the mind creates a need to look for a centre, and perpetuates the illusion that it exists.

An incident relating to J. Krishnamurti illustrates the relationship between the principles and the way that they regulate our lives at three different levels. A few years before his death, there was a fire which damaged his apartment at Brockwood Park, in England. Krishnamurti was for me an archetypal figure and I wrote to a friend about this incident mentioning that I thought there must have been some problem with his liver. I had been reminded of Prometheus stealing fire for the earth and consequently having his liver devoured by an eagle. For me, Krishnamurti was expressing the principle of vibration in his talks, especially when he spoke of the observer being the observed, and beyond that he was facilitating both through his presence and his teaching an extraordinary form of communication that took place between the higher aspects of my being and the lower self. Krishnamurti died two years later of cancer of the liver and pancreas, the area of the body where the principle of correspondence is reflected. I personally felt that he had simply withdrawn the energies from the planes of matter, time and space, translating the harmonics of his being - correspondence, vibration, communication/communion - to abide in other dimensions.

Imagine that you are at a firework display and there is a light going up into the night sky. Suddenly there is an explosion and a big ball of light appears out of that little point of light. The point of light could be compared to the Big Bang and the ball of light to the energy field that instantaneously came into being. Or the point of light could be the moment of conception with the ball of light being the formation of a new entity immediately subject to the universal principles, and regulated by the universal laws. The point of light is represented in the figure at point A. Within this sphere of light, let us draw the three triangles as shown below, creating a form of enneagram with each angle touching the circumference at nine equidistant points representing each of the nine principles. The point at the centre of the sphere represents the moment of creation, and for us it is conception, from which everything which is manifest will issue.

The enneagram can be compared to a mobile constantly moving on a pivot, the point A. One of the principles, represented by one of the angles of one of the triangles gives you the energy you require at any particular moment to express your humanness, and is replaced by another one as that need is fulfilled and new ones arise.

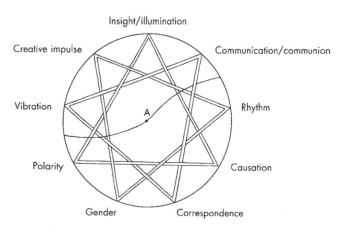

Insight/illumination
Creative impulse
Communication/communion
Vibration
A
Rhythm
Polarity
Causation
Gender
Correspondence

The Enneagram

Let us now draw a line separating the principles at work in time, space and matter from those at work out of time, space and matter, forming two domains. As we work with any one principle (see the next chapter on the practice) we work within the dynamism of a group that includes at least one principle which is at work in the other domain, producing a state of great balance and harmony.

With the first triangle (see Figure 1) we have two principles operating in time, space and matter - causation and polarity - and one principle operating out of time, space and matter - insight/illumination. With the second triangle (see Figure 2) we have one principle operating in time, space and matter – correspondence – and two principles operating out of time, space and matter – vibration and communication/communion. With the third triangle (see Figure 3) we have gender and rhythm operating in time, space and matter and creative impulse operating out of time, space and matter.

The principle of correspondence has a function in time, space and matter that is most consequential. It is connected with, and reflects, the energies of the principles of communication/communion and of vibration, the domain of both of which is out of time, space and matter. Of the five principles that exercise their influence in time, space and matter, correspondence is the only one that has correlative affinities with two universal principles at work out of time, space and matter. The other four have affinities, and receive energies from, one principle at work in time, space and matter and one principle at work out of time, space and matter. This is of vital importance because of the transfer of influences from the principle of causation to the principle of correspondence which is taking place at the moment.

Returning to the triad as opposed to the triangles, direction seems to be involved in the manner in which these principles came to be reflected in specific parts of the human body. In the triad – gender, causation and correspondence – the base of the body and the base of the spine reflect the feminine and the masculine aspects of our being, with which we "cause" something new, and causation is reflected in the sexual organs. That which has been caused opens to the world and this is reflected in the solar plexus where we also find the principle of correspondence. The direction is one of evolution, from the bottom upwards, connected to the parts of the body which are below the diaphragm in human beings.

The second triad is that of vibration, polarity and rhythm where the direction is from top to bottom. These three principles have a subtler element pertaining to them because one of them, the Principle of Vibration, is operating out of time, space and matter. It goes from the "bridge" of light between the pineal and the pituitary glands to the diaphragm. I like to compare the principle of vibration to a balloon that expands as it is blown up and contracts as the air is let out. Any point on the inner wall is connected, as it were, to its opposite point. They are interdependent, the points being the poles. The movement from one point to its opposite point is that of rhythm.

The principle of creative impulse is part of the third triad, this one with all three principles at work totally out of time, space and matter. In these ethereal realms, in the domain of unity, it is questionable whether we can talk of direction. From the standpoint of our subjective consciousness, however, we could say that the direction is from the bottom upwards. I like to compare the action of the principle of creative impulse to that of two weather fronts. We know already that there are two aspects to the action of the principle of creative impulse: the vertical feedback and the horizontal feedback. In one way, these two feedback movements are opposites. One is connected with total creativity and the other with destruction, with maintaining the *status quo*. Although I compared the action of the creative impulse to that of two weather fronts, we are now in the level of unity, out of time, space and matter. So these two weather fronts are continuously coming up against each other. The direction with these last three Principles appears to be from the bottom upwards - weather fronts (creative impulse) meeting and creating the flash of lightning (insight/illumination) which lights up all the heavens (communication/ communion). The metaphor is worth entertaining!

I would like now to look at another phenomenon connected with the three triads. We have already seen that they are separated by lines, as it were, of the bridge of light between the pineal and the pituitary glands, and the diaphragm. Let us apply these lines to our enneagram to separate the three groups of triads. We have seen that there are specific directions to the establishment of the different triads of the principles and we can put an arrow at both ends of the two lines. We can now see that as we extend the two lines, one end of each of them will meet at a point while their opposite ends will go to infinity. The point where they meet can be compared to alpha and their other ends to omega. "I am Alpha and Omega, the beginning and the ending."[62] This is the definition of infinity. The sign of infinity is the figure of eight. If we look at the diaphragm from underneath we see that the muscles are disposed horizontally in a figure of eight. Do we carry within ourselves the sign of infinity? The diaphragm is recognised as the active power behind breathing; could the breath be our bridge to infinity?

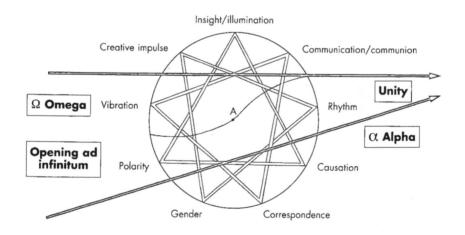

The esoteric definition of an enneagram as given by Ouspensky is: "A certain symbol which points out the method of cognising of a thing examined in itself"[63]. Another definition could be: a symbol that contains within itself the energy of its own definition. When we study the enneagram it can reveal its meaning to us. Symbols are tools that we can use to have an intimation of unity. The extraordinary dynamism of the enneagram, like that of a mandala provides the energy that can enable us to tune in to different dimensions.

Sitting in contemplation of the enneagram of the nine principles triggered many insights for me. The work with the Universal Principles which I discuss in the next chapter is the application of these insights.

CHAPTER ELEVEN

An understanding of the transition from animal consciousness to human consciousness is revealed in myths and fables from all over the world, from the Popol Vuh of the Ancient Quiché Maya to the Christian Bible, to name but a few. The young baby is still manifesting the level at which humans like animals are simply conscious. Very soon the step up in consciousness normally occurs as one becomes aware that one is aware, moving from Adam and Eve's paradise to the toil and sweat of the world of duality. Being in the world, with access to the fuel of matter we are able to reveal our true nature from who we are – body, mind, emotion, personality - to what we are; beings of light cloaked in matter subject to time and space. In the Oneness of the Light we can express the thoughts that inform us, guided by the cosmic intelligence that we really are, whose purpose is to reveal to us our greatness, grandeur and beauty.

The Universe is simple in design and yet extremely complex in its manifestation of that design. The design is both the designer and the manifestations. That is why the moment of our conception contains all the elements necessary for the revelation of our true nature and through that moment we can reach out to the Universal Mind which manifests itself with an order that is recognised in the Universal Principles. As we have seen these regulate all levels of existence and we can access them through the specific parts of the body where they are reflected, namely the feet, the hands and the head.

The Practice

You can work with the Universal Principles wherever you are, at any time of day. There are no special requirements. The person you are working with and whom I will call the client may be watching television, reading a book, lying in bed or simply doing nothing. If they fall asleep then just carry on until you have finished. Babies and young children will indicate the end of a session by pulling their feet away. Some people like to talk during the session, others go into a deep relaxation, it makes no difference. If you are talking with them, however, be careful not to get involved in diagnosis. Let your hands get on with touching the feet, hands and head while you remain detached. The state of the client makes no difference to the work.

To give a session with the Universal Principles, you need to do two things only: one at the mental level, one at the physical. At the mental level you need only say inwardly from time to time: Universal Principles. You are thus aligning yourself to their dynamism. You need not name each principle as you touch the corresponding areas where they are reflected on the feet, the hands and the head.

At the physical level, the procedure is as follows: the moment of conception is our reference point, which is the moment when the Principles start manifesting. This is why, when we are working with the Universal Principles, we touch lightly with one finger, with a small circular or vibratory movement the point of conception which is reflected on the sides of the first articulation of the big toe, the sides of the first articulation of the thumb and at the top of the head where the fontanel is to be found with young babies. With the other hand, we touch the specific parts of the feet, hands and head that reflect the Principles.

The Feet

Sit with your client opposite or at right angles to you with his foot comfortably on your lap. You can place a small cloth under the foot if you wish as at times the foot may start sweating. We usually start with the right foot. Place your hands over the foot and pause for a moment before you take hold of it, giving yourself the time to leave behind the thoughts of the day and giving the client time to adjust to your presence. State simply in yourself your intention of working with the Universal Principles.

Then take the foot firmly with both hands and begin to get acquainted with it, letting your hands roam freely for a few minutes over the foot and the ankle. Having a firm touch does away with any feelings of ticklishness, which is merely superficial tension. Remember that you are working not just with the foot but with the whole person, so let your consciousness be aware that the condition of the foot is a reflection of the client's overall state of being and do not attempt to diagnose or think of changing anything. In this way you are fulfilling the mind's yearning to gather information. Simply observe and move on. You have acknowledged the client in their totality.

Remember that our reference point is the moment of

conception and begin the session by touching with one hand the sides of the first articulation of the big toe while the thumb and fingers of your other hand move up and down the spinal reflexes from the big toe to the heel. Imagine a line along the bony ridge on the inside of the foot. Allow your fingers to move wherever they want to along this line, following the bone rather than the curve of the soft tissue. The intelligence in your fingers is far more in tune with what needs to be done than your mind is, so let them be your guide. Use any fingers you want to, with the movement or pressure you feel comfortable with. The movements in your two hands can, for instance, be circular, probing, or vibratory, as if you were playing a tiny cello. You may find the pressure changing from very light to quite firm with different fingers coming into use at different times. Just do whatever feels right, without attempting to shift energy blockages or crystal deposits if you meet some.

You are not giving a massage and you are not attempting to bring about change, physical or otherwise. It is like a dance of your fingers. We are working in a non-involved and non-invasive way, so allow the hands complete freedom of movement, up and down the spinal reflex area, in a relaxed and gentle way.

Work all over the outside edge of the big toe, paying attention to the upper and lower corners of the nail, which are the reflex points of the pineal and pituitary glands respectively. Then, from the joint of the big toe, the reflex point of conception, follow the bony ridge. Notice the groove between the cuneiform and the navicular bones, as shown on the chart. Move onto the calcaneum under the ankle bone and touch the whole of the side of the heel area to the point where the Achilles tendon attaches. Work only on the bone and, at the heel, on the padded area to the side, where it is difficult at times to feel the bone. Work up and down this line at will. Occasionally work from under the inner ankle bone, across the top of the foot, to under the outer ankle bone. There is no fixed starting or finishing point.

As you work, the client may well say that some areas feel painful, or you may gradually come to notice that some areas feel sticky or blocked. Just acknowledge this and then let the knowledge go. Do not try and work on these areas more than others, nor avoid them. Touch the whole foot in the same way. Reassure the client that he need not worry if his feet go to sleep! This is usually

Chart of the Universal Principles as formulated by Gaston Saint-Pierre

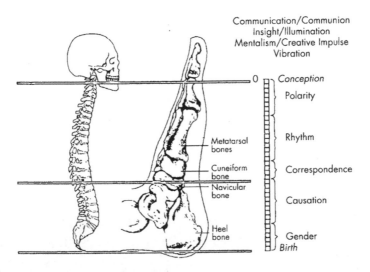

Communication/Communion
Insight/Illumination
Mentalism/Creative Impulse
Vibration

0 — Conception

Polarity

Metatarsal bones — Rhythm

Cuneiform bone — Correspondence
Navicular bone

Causation

Heel bone — Gender
Birth

simply due to a temporary lack of circulation.

After approximately 20 to 30 minutes, stroke the foot all over to finish. You can work with your hands a little away from the foot, without touching it, for a few minutes if you want to, following along the bony ridge.

Then use the same procedure on the other foot. After both feet have been worked on, wash your hands in cold water, which does not open the pores, to remove any excess energy you may have picked up from the client's feet.

The Principles are reflected on the feet in the following areas:

The point of conception is reflected on the sides of the first articulation of the big toe and must be touched all the time with a slight circular or vibratory movement.

Principle of Gender—the side of the heel bone to the point where the Achilles tendon attaches itself to the bone.

Principle of Causation—below the ankle bone on the side of the heel bone and across the ankle, to below the outer ankle bone.

Principle of Correspondence—the side of the navicular and cuneiform bones, where little indentations or grooves can be found.

Principle of Rhythm—from the second articulation or joint of the big toe all along the side of the metatarsal bone.

Principle of Polarity—from the first to the second articulation, on the side of the second phalanx of the big toe.

Principle of Vibration—lower corners of the nail—pituitary gland reflex points.

Principle of Creative Impulse—upper corners of the nail—pineal gland reflex point.

Principle of Insight/Illumination and Principle of Communication/Communion—as these Principles are supra human they are not reflected in the body as such and so we touch the point of conception while aligning ourselves to their energies and their dynamism, simply by naming them from time to time within ourselves.

The Hands

Sit next to your client, and place her right hand on a cushion covered by a small cloth on your lap or theirs. I have found that the cushion provides an objective structure to work from which counteracts the intimacy that may embarrass the client.

At the mental level, say in yourself from time to time: Universal Principles. At the physical level, with one hand hold the sides of the first articulation of the thumb and with the other hand, follow a medial line down the outside edge always along the bony ridge from the top of the thumb down to the wrist. Work across the back of the wrist occasionally as you did across the ankle. Do each hand for 5-10 minutes, or longer if the client wishes.

The Universal Principles are reflected on the side of the thumb in the following areas:

The point of conception is reflected on the sides of the first knuckle and must be touched lightly all the time, with small circular or vibratory movements.

Principle of Gender—the place where the thumb goes into the wrist and across the top of the wrist.

Principle of Causation—from the second knuckle to the base of the wrist along the bony ridge.

Principle of Correspondence—on the side of the second knuckle.

Principle of Rhythm—just above the second knuckle.

Principle of Polarity—just below the first knuckle.

Principle of Vibration—lower corners of the nail.

Principle of Creative impulse—top corners of the nail.

The Principle of Insight/Illumination and the Principle

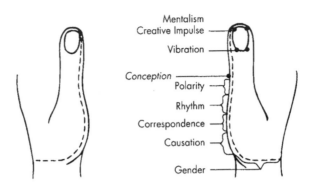

Chart of the hands

of Communication/Communion—again as these Principles are supra human they are not reflected in the body as such which is why we touch the point of conception only while aligning ourselves to their energies and their dynamism, simply by naming them from time to time within ourselves.

The Head

Seat the client in an upright chair and stand behind her. Extremely lightly, touch with one finger the top of the head where the fontanel was situated as a young baby, as this reflects the moment of conception. With the other hand, work with a small circular or vibratory movement from the top of the head to the base of the skull along a medial line. Lift the fingers as you work from one point to another so that they do not pull the hair. The touch must be very gentle. Also go along the base of the skull, following the occipital ridge up to the mastoid bones immediately behind the ears, then move behind, and up to, the top of the ears. The head can be worked on for 10 minutes or longer. The client usually feels pleasantly relaxed, so do not disturb her afterwards, rather leave her alone for a few minutes while you wash your hands in cold water. After any session, allow your clients time and space to be quiet, if that is what they want to do.

The Principles are reflected on the head at the following places:

Principle of Gender – all along the occipital ridge at the base of the skull, about the area that can be touched with an open hand.

Principle of Causation – from the atlas upwards along a central line perpendicular to the occipital ridge at the back of the head, an area covered by about four fingers.

Principle of Correspondence – the area of the crown covered by two fingers.

Principle of Rhythm—the width of two or three fingers above and in front of the crown.

Principle of Polarity—the width of two or three fingers just behind the point of conception.

Principle of Vibration—the width of one finger just in front of the point of conception.

Principle of Creative Impulse—the width of one finger

in front of the area reflecting the Principle of Vibration.

Principle of Insight/Illumination and Principle of Communication/Communion— again, as with the hands and feet, we touch the point of conception while naming them from time to time within ourselves.

You can see that the actual session is very easy to give: a simple touch on the spinal reflexes along the inner bony ridge of the feet and around the top of the ankles, and along the bony ridge of the thumbs and across the top of the wrists, along the centre line of the skull, along the base of the skull and up to the ears. How many sessions should be given is more difficult to say and this is really only something the client can know. They may want only one or they may wish to continue for several weeks or months. They may decide to come for a number of consecutive weeks, and then every other week, or once a

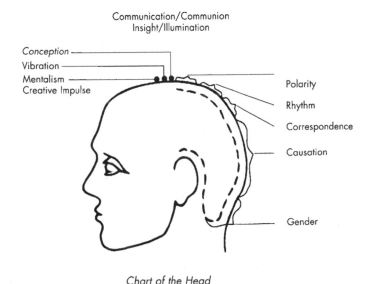

Chart of the Head

month, for example. The life force within knows what they need and they must have the space in which to make their own decisions. Clients choose their practitioner and decide the frequency of their visits, through discovering and exercising their own inner authority. It is not up to the practitioner to decide.

We discussed in the last chapter how each principle belongs to a family of three principles, at least one of which operates in the domain out of time, space and matter. The mind is a tool that consciousness has fashioned in order to function in time, space and matter, in duality and as such the mind cannot exercise its will at the level of unity, out of time, space and matter, will power being simply a convergence of forces brought about by the mind to accomplish something. Whereas detachment is important if our creativity is to flourish, it is present per se when we work with the Universal Principles. This means that the precautions which have to be taken to ensure that the mind is bypassed when you are working with approaches such as the Metamorphic Technique are no longer necessary. Such a deep state of balance is established between the two domains – the one in and the other out of time space and matter, that two persons can give each other sessions with the Universal Principles at the same time, facing one another, without a closed circuit of energy being formed. We can also, if we wish, receive sessions every day without confusion arising because the mind with its low frequency simply cannot fathom what is happening in terms of the transformation of patterns. The ability to integrate changes is thus at its peak.

The underlying purpose of the work with the Universal Principles is transformation. We use the mind and the fingers to help develop an attitude that acts as a catalyst in the creation of an environment, free of direction, in which the life force of the client, guided by their innate intelligence, may fulfil their highest potential.

Is there a difference between the work with the Metamorphic Technique and the one with the Universal Principles? The whole subject is one of transformation. There are therefore two approaches to Metamorphosis within our particular discipline: there is the exoteric one which includes the Metamorphic Technique, and which can be taught to, and practised by, everyone, even children and people with learning difficulties. I have showed the practice on the feet to ten children in the classroom of a Montessori school where I taught for a time. Within a few minutes they had entered a deep silence from which they emerged 30 minutes later, peaceful and content. The next day I taught them the practice on the hands and the head. They went on giving each other sessions as and when they felt like it. Wonderful breakthroughs happened especially with two of them.

I have also taught people with learning difficulties to give each other sessions; again there came the feeling that intelligence was at last evoked. The two prerequisites of the work were present with these and the children: the person receiving the session is alive and the practitioner is detached (at least their mind is not attempting to impose a direction).

The esoteric approach, the Universal Principles, needs the mind to recognise that the universe is regulated by laws, and the tool of the mind is not yet developed in children or exercised in people with learning difficulties. Such people would find it hard to practise with the second approach – that of the Universal Principles - as it is more esoteric and the mind has a different role to play, as the two aspects of our nature, in and out of time, space and matter are evoked.

Within the context of the two approaches of the Metamorphic Technique and the Universal Principles, the attitude of mind of the practitioner being of detachment allows for the emergence of a feeling of unity. This manifests at the physical level as the practitioner's fingers and the client's feet, hands or head merge to become one energy. Even animals respond to this approach and may enter into a state of suspension despite great pain or suffering. It is a diving into the very unity, which we are from our origin. Duality ceases. The energies are one. This is communication, a partaking in the objective lovingness of the one Power.

CHAPTER TWELVE

The value of the Metamorphic Technique is gaining increasing recognition in Europe, Australia and elsewhere throughout the world. Since the launch of The Metamorphic Association in 1979 countless people have benefited from the way it seems to facilitate the movement of transformation and self-healing, particularly within family groups. Moreover it has been introduced successfully to a number of institutional settings, such as homes and organisations for autistic children and children with Down's Syndrome, and also in psychiatric institutions, stroke rehabilitation centres and so on.

The Universal Principles are a recent development within The Metamorphic Technique, increasingly used by practitioners separately or integrated into their existing practice. The Metamorphic Technique, as I explained very briefly in the Introduction, emerged in the 1970s as a radical development of reflexology and what was then known as pre-natal therapy. One of the basic principles is the belief that every individual is profoundly affected by patterns and influences that are precipitated into the first cell at the moment of their conception, and ingrained in the foetus during the gestation period. Much of our lives is spent, often in conflict, living out the repercussions of these patterns. The Metamorphic Technique somehow seems to bring our consciousness to bear on these early configurations, and people who experience it sometimes gain a sense of release from destructive patterns of behaviour that may have dogged them all their lives.

One of the underlying problems that frequently emerge

to the light during a series of Metamorphic sessions is a basic disequilibrium within ourselves. Some people tend to display an over-developed sense of individuality, of awareness of their thinking process. They may become isolated, lost in their own heads, slow to care for others' needs. The opposite is the case with people whose moving, emotive, reactive energies are well-developed: they may tend to act before thinking, or find it hard to envisage the consequences of their actions. It is likely that the "thinking" centre is primarily nurtured and developed in the first half of pregnancy, and the "moving" centre in the second half. An individual is likely to be far more healthy, balanced, happy, and fulfilled if these centres are more or less harmonised.

With the Universal Principles, we approach an underlying duality at an even more fundamental level. We believe that we are beings of light, clothed in matter; that we are souls embedded in bodies. This fact has been expressed in world religions and mysticism since the beginning of recorded history. Indeed one may say that a central concern of most systems of mysticism has been to transcend the flesh and liberate the spirit; to come to an understanding of our true spiritual nature; to gain a vision of God and the heavenly realms, and end our fascination with the materialising influences of the world. Techniques such as yoga, meditation, ritual, and asceticism all tend - more or less successfully - towards this goal. A universal vision is our birthright. However, because of our self-imposed restrictions it seems that we live in a gaol. The poet William Blake expresses it perfectly: "If the doors of perception were cleansed, everything would appear to man as it is, infinite. For man has closed himself up, till he sees all things thro' the narrow chinks of his cavern."[64]

In our work with the Universal Principles we often use the terminology "in (or out) of time, space, and matter" to refer to the two realms. These terms were also used by mystics of the past. Blake again wrote that "the Visions of Eternity, by reason of narrowed perceptions, Are become weak Visions of Time and Space, fix'd into furrows of death"; and we find in the works of Swami Vivekananda: "Time, space, and causation are like the glass through which the Absolute is seen, and when It is seen on the lower side, It appears as the universe. In the Absolute there is neither time, space, nor causation. What we call causation begins after the degeneration of the Absolute into the phenomenal."[65]

By learning about the dynamics of, and the connections between the two domains, we aim to develop an ease of movement within and between them. At the highest level, we may come to the understanding that we are indeed beings of light; that light and intelligence are our source and always at our disposal, and yet we are clothed in matter - which we can consciously embrace and enjoy in its own terms. As we have seen, four of the nine principles, namely Communication/Communion, Insight/Illumination, Creative Impulse and Vibration are in the realm out of time, space and matter while the other five, Polarity, Rhythm, Correspondence, Causation and Gender relate to our normal world. The Principle of Vibration exercises the greatest influence in both domains and is thus something of a boundary-crosser. Because the principles appear to form in "family groups" we often get a feeling of resonance with the domain out of time, space, and matter even while we are working with the lower group.

We have adopted the work with the feet, hands, and head from The Metamorphic Technique. These specific parts of the body have been found to have a marvellous, and inexplicable, capacity to act as a kind of support in matter for transformation. They are like a canvas on which a unique piece of art can be painted, allowing metamorphosis from conflict to harmony, and from darkness to light. Touch on the feet, hands, and head basically constitutes a kind of ritual, which could be compared to the rituals of Buddhism, Hinduism or indeed to the ritual of Holy Communion in Christianity, where wine and bread are tasted to invoke the living presence of the Christ. In much ritual, the officiant requires many religious trappings. With The Metamorphic Technique each of us performs a living ritual, and the requirements are not external but constituted of our own bodies.

The outcome of sessions with the Metamorphic Technique and the Universal Principles is immeasurable and unpredictable and very often imperceptible to the person concerned. There is often an increased awareness, with people becoming brighter, perhaps more decisive. As their consciousness evolves or transmutes, so they may attract and create a different environment: old patterns of working, relating, or consuming may no longer have relevance to their new level of consciousness, and thus they fall away naturally. This process appears to be life enhancing and fruitful although at times it can be quite rapid and even disturbing. The life-force is not always respectful of convention. The use of the Universal Principles in sessions provokes the two sides of our nature, that in as well as that out of time, space and matter. We have found that the movement of. transformation elicits even more profound and balanced changes in people than those which occur if the Metamorphic Technique is used.

One insight that is gained through these practices is that we are constantly in the presence of perfection. Everything in our environment - our spouse, our children, our boss, our home - is a wonderfully exact representation of the configuration of our consciousness. We create a *perfect* image of ourselves in our surroundings. It is an inescapable consequence that, as we change, our environment changes too. We do not need to make any effort: indeed, effort may only slow the process.

However, there will come periods when there is a time lag between the new "you" and your surroundings. Consciousness moves at a faster rate of vibration than matter does, and your level of awareness may change more rapidly than your physical structure. When that happens, you may experience a feeling of being caught in a kind of void: not the true, shining, luminous void of the mystics, but a disturbing sense of disorientation, where things seem to make no sense. A symptom of this state may be weird and indecipherable dreams which I believe suggest that the old patterns of consciousness in the brain are trying - and failing - to interpret the new energies. In my experience, this void is to be welcomed as a sign that we are moving along an exciting path of discovery. As we surrender to the new energies and move to new levels of consciousness, this void of confusion will give way to the true void.

The true void is a gift from life, free and without determination, pure and without direction. Without our looking for it or desiring it, it arises, precipitated by grace which is the means that objective love uses to communicate. Grace then dissolves the activities of thought, memory and direction, working in such an intimate and silent way that you believe that you are empty because there appears to be no movement, nothing seems to be happening.

Through this void we may reach out to the light of love in the heart where the void is made fertile. The light of love is first experienced as an all-consuming and destructive fire. Imagine if you were to dive into the heart of the sun; you would be annihilated and the light would disappear. Then through that dark night, your whole being starts to radiate in ever more subtle vibration, uniting, resonating, and harmonising with the light of life. There is oneness.

NOTES

Chapter 1

[1] *Androgyny* by Lorna St. Aubyn, Published in *Metamorphosis, The Journal of the Metamorphic Association.* No. 10 Pages 30-31 Autumn 1986

[2] *New Science of Life* by Rupert Sheldrake, publisher Anthony Blond 1981.

[3] *"Universal laws or universal habits"* by Eddie O'Brien. Published in *Metamorphosis, The Journal of the Metamorphic Association.* No. 10 Pages 27-28 Autumn 1986.

[4] *Universal laws or universal habits* by Eddie O'Brien. Published in *Metamorphosis, The Journal of the Metamorphic Association.* No. 10 Pages 27-28 Autumn 1986.

Chapter 2

[5] *Insight on Conception* by Alan Hunter. Published in *Metamorphosis, The Journal of the Metamorphic Association.* No. 9 Pages 7-10 Summer 1986.

[6] Published in *Metamorphosis, The Journal of the Metamorphic Association.* No. 11 Page 5 Winter/Spring 1987.

[7] *Insight on Conception* by Alan Hunter. Published in *Metamorphosis, The Journal of the Metamorphic Association.* " No. 9 Pages 7-10 Summer 1986.

[8] John 8,9.

Chapter 3

[9] *Geophysical Upheaval* by Mark Tolson. Published in *Metamorphosis. The Journal of the Metamorphic Association.* No. 10 Page 15 Autumn 1986.

[10] *The Metamorphic Technique* by Gaston Saint-Pierre and Debbie Shapiro. Published by Vega.

[11] *The Metamorphic Technique* by Gaston Saint-Pierre and Debbie Shapiro. Published by Vega. Page 9.

[12] ibid.

[13] *The Universal Law of Correspondences* by Michael Stanley. The Swedenborg Movement Leaflet No. 10. The Swedenborg Society, 20/21 Bloomsbury Way, London WC1 2TH. England. Page 2.

[14] ibid. page 5.

[15] *The Metamorphic Technique* by Gaston Saint-Pierre and Debbie Shapiro. Published by Vega.

[16] *Mat* 12:48

[17] *The Lazy Man's Guide to Enlightenment* by Thaddeus Golas. Published by Bantam Books Inc. 1980. Page 45.

Chapter 4

[18] *Starseed, the third millennium: living in the posthistoric world* by Ken Carey. Harper San Francisco. 1991. Page 47.

[19] *The Sufi Message of Hazrat Inayat Khan*, Vol.II. Pub. for International Headquarters of the Sufi Movement, Geneva, by Barrie and Rockliff, London, 1960.

[20] *The Interior Realization* by Hubert Benoit, Element Books, 1987.

[21] *Four Quartets*, T.S. Eliot, *Collected Poems 1909-1962*, Faber and Faber, 1963.

[22] *Prenatal Origin of Genius*, Bernard, 1986.

[23] *The New Scientist*, 25 July 1985.

[24] *Newsweek*, 12 January 1987.

[25] *Starseed, the third millennium: living in the posthistoric world* by Ken Carey. Harper San Francisco. 1991. Page 14.

[26] *The Sufi Message of Hazrat Inayat Khan*, Vol.II. Pub. for International Headquarters of the Sufi Movement, Geneva, by Barrie and Rockliff, London, 1960.

[27] *The Lazy Man's Guide to Enlightenment* by Thaddeus Golas. Published by Bantam Books Inc. 1980. Page 21.

[28] *The Lazy Man's Guide to Enlightenment* by Thaddeus Golas. Published by Bantam Books Inc. 1980. Page 17.

Chapter 5

[29] *The Lazy Man's Guide to Enlightenment* by Thaddeus Golas. Published by Bantam Books Inc. 1980. Page 37.

[30] *Polarity* by Jean Freer. Published in *Metamorphosis, The Journal of the Metamorphic Association.* No. 14 Page 26. Winter/Spring 1988.

[31] *Starseed, the third millennium: living in the posthistoric world* by Ken Carey. Harper San Francisco. 1991. Pages 9-10.

Chapter 6

[32] *Starseed, the third millennium: living in the posthistoric world* by Ken Carey. Harper San Francisco. 1991. Page 10.

[33] *The Lazy Man's Guide to Enlightenment* by Thaddeus Golas. Published by Bantam Books Inc. 1980. Page 16.

[34] *Starseed, the third millennium: living in the posthistoric world* by Ken Carey. Harper San Francisco. 1991. Page 32.

[35] *Starseed, the third millennium: living in the posthistoric world* by Ken Carey. Harper San Francisco. 1991. Page 160.

[36] *The Lazy Man's Guide to Enlightenment* by Thaddeus Golas. Published by Bantam Books Inc. 1980. Pages 13-14.

[37] Ibid. Page 19.

[38] Hazrat Inayat Khan.

[39] *The Great Gospel of John* by Jacob Lorber. Published by Lorber Verlag. 1984.

[40] *Starseed, the third millennium: living in the posthistoric world* by Ken Carey. Harper San Francisco. 1991. Page 153.

[41] *Starseed, the third millennium: living in the posthistoric world* by Ken Carey. Harper San Francisco. 1991. Page 164.

[42] *Blueprint for immortality. The Electric Patterns of Life* by Harold Saxton Burr. Neville Spearman Publishers 1972.

[43] That type of attention seems to inhibit a function of the pituitary gland that has to do with the release of enzymes that regulate the threshold of pain that one can endure.

[44] Life - Metamorphosis - Change by Gaston Saint-Pierre. Published in *Metamorphosis, The Journal of the Metamorphic Association*. No. 19 Pages 45-50 Autumn 1989.

Chapter 7

[45] *The Mistress of Vision* by Francis Thompson quoted in George Trevelyan's book: *Magic Casements*. Published by Coventure Limited. London 1980.

[46] *Starseed, the third millennium: living in the posthistoric world* by Ken Carey. Harper San Francisco. 1991. Page 35.

[47] *The Song of a Man who has Come Through* quoted in George Trevelyan's book: *Magic Casements*. Published by Coventure Limited. London 1980.

[48] (Lecture topics: The Pineal Gland as the Third Eye or Psychic Chakra).

[49] *New Scientist* 25 July 1985, page 43.

Chapter 8

[50] The Gospel according to Matthew 10: 34.

[51] *Metamorphosis, The Journal of the Metamorphic Association*. No. 11. Interview with Dr. David Bohm "The power of concept" Winter/Spring 1987. Page 6.

[52] *Exploration into Insight* by Krishnamurti, Harper and Row Publishers, pages 44 - 46.

[53] ibid.

[54] *The Starseed Transmissions - An Extraterrestrial Report* by Ken Carey, Uni-Sun Publishers, pages 46-47.

[55] *Vision* by Ken Carey, Publishing Ltd., page 65.

[56] *Le Mental des cellules*, by Satprem, Robert Laffont Publishers - Paris, pages 146-147.

Chapter 9

[57] The Gospel according to Matthew 22: 36-40.

[58] The Gospel according to Matthew 17: 20.

[59] *The Challenge of Fate*, by Thorwarld Dethlefsen, Coventure Ltd, London page 142.

[60] *Starseed, the third millennium: living in the posthistoric world* by Ken Carey. Harper San Francisco. 1991. Page 91.

Chapter 10

[61] *The Metamorphic Technique* by Gaston Saint-Pierre and Debbie Shapiro. Published by Vega.

[62] *St. John's Revelations,* i.7

[63] *In search of the miraculous* by Ouspenski.

Chapter 12

[64] William Blake, *The Marriage of Heaven and Hell,* Plate 14 in *The Complete Writings of William Blake* (edited by Geoffrey Keynes, London: Oxford University Press, 1966), p. 154.

[65] Swami Vivekananda, *Jnana Yoga,* (5th edn, Calcutta, Advaita Ashrama, 1997), p. 109.

For more information on workshops and lectures, contact Gaston Saint-Pierre at 67 Ritherdon Road, London SW17 8QE.

Email: stpierregaston@aol.com.

You may also be interested in consulting the Metamorphic Association's website at www.metamorphicAssociation.org.uk